2024 C...

JANUARY
M	T	W	T	F	S	S
1	2	3	4	5	6	7
8	9	10	11	12	13	14
15	16	17	18	19	20	21
22	23	24	25	26	27	28
29	30	31				

FEBRUARY
M	T	W	T	F	S	S
			1	2	3	4
5	6	7	8	9	10	11
12	13	14	15	16	17	18
19	20	21	22	23	24	25
26	27	28	29			

MARCH
M	T	W	T	F	S	S
				1	2	3
4	5	6	7	8	9	10
11	12	13	14	15	16	17
18	19	20	21	22	23	24
25	26	27	28	29	30	31

APRIL
M	T	W	T	F	S	S
1	2	3	4	5	6	7
8	9	10	11	12	13	14
15	16	17	18	19	20	21
22	23	24	25	26	27	28
29	30					

MAY
M	T	W	T	F	S	S
		1	2	3	4	5
6	7	8	9	10	11	12
13	14	15	16	17	18	19
20	21	22	23	24	25	26
27	28	29	30	31		

JUNE
M	T	W	T	F	S	S
					1	2
3	4	5	6	7	8	9
10	11	12	13	14	15	16
17	18	19	20	21	22	23
24	25	26	27	28	29	30

JULY
M	T	W	T	F	S	S
1	2	3	4	5	6	7
8	9	10	11	12	13	14
15	16	17	18	19	20	21
22	23	24	25	26	27	28
29	30	31				

AUGUST
M	T	W	T	F	S	S
			1	2	3	4
5	6	7	8	9	10	11
12	13	14	15	16	17	18
19	20	21	22	23	24	25
26	27	28	29	30	31	

SEPTEMBER
M	T	W	T	F	S	S
						1
2	3	4	5	6	7	8
9	10	11	12	13	14	15
16	17	18	19	20	21	22
23	24	25	26	27	28	29
30						

OCTOBER
M	T	W	T	F	S	S
	1	2	3	4	5	6
7	8	9	10	11	12	13
14	15	16	17	18	19	20
21	22	23	24	25	26	27
28	29	30	31			

NOVEMBER
M	T	W	T	F	S	S
				1	2	3
4	5	6	7	8	9	10
11	12	13	14	15	16	17
18	19	20	21	22	23	24
25	26	27	28	29	30	

DECEMBER
M	T	W	T	F	S	S
						1
2	3	4	5	6	7	8
9	10	11	12	13	14	15
16	17	18	19	20	21	22
23	24	25	26	27	28	29
30	31					

ACKNOWLEDGEMENTS

I'm so excited to be able to bring you another new diary. It actually never gets old for me, this weaving and creation of a magical companion each year that we can all use together.

This diary is for you who come along each year and catch the flow of the cycles.

Every year my gratitude extends to my husband Adam and my agent Richard Martin for their ongoing support and presence. As always, a joyful thank you for the amazing cover art of Kinga Britschigi and a thank you to my publisher Lisa Hanrahan and her team at Rockpool Publishing.

As always this work is dedicated, as it has been since the very first edition, to my patroness, the goddess Artemis. I first loved you as a small child and my love has only grown since.

Stacey Demarco

2024 LUNAR

& SEASONAL DIARY

NORTHERN HEMISPHERE

ROCKPOOL
rockpoolpublishing.com

We are members of one great
body, planted by nature.
— Seneca, Stoic philosopher, 4 BCE – 65 CE

A Rockpool book
PO Box 252 Summer Hill
NSW 2130
Australia
rockpoolpublishing.com
Follow us! **f** 🄾 rockpoolpublishing
Tag your images with #rockpoolpublishing

ISBN 978-1-925946-66-6
Northern hemisphere edition

Published in 2023 by Rockpool Publishing
Copyright text © Stacey Demarco, 2023
Copyright design © Rockpool Publishing, 2023
Design by Sara Lindberg, Rockpool Publishing
Typeset by Daniel Poole, Rockpool Publishing
Cover design by Kinga Britschgi
Edited by Lisa Macken
Author photo by Jason Corroto
Images from Shutterstock

Printed and bound in China
10 9 8 7 6 5 4 3 2 1

HOW TO USE THIS DIARY

Welcome to a new year and a diary with a difference!

I am writing this under a big, fat, almost full moon. I'm lying on a soft blanket in my garden with a pen and notebook and the moon is lighting my way, such is its bright illumination. The stars are there twinkling but I see the planets even more distinctly tonight, so the sky looks deep and infinite.

The Norse had a special word for this sitting out, *utiseta*, and it was used as both a meditative act and also meant to lie upon the earth as a conduit between the night sky and the ancestors who had walked the earth before us. Tonight, though, I am not just connecting with you all in this future writing but I'm also taking in the alchemy of the moonlight, the starlight and the plants and animals of the darkness.

In my own garden, you see, I have purposefully grown plants of the night to magnify my moon experience. I am sitting near my night-flowering jasmine, which of course smells lush and lovely, and this is mixed on the breeze with night-blooming honeysuckle. I have Japanese wisteria, datura, angel's trumpet, moonflowers and gardenia – all of which are at their best at night. I am waiting on a large cactus, called queen of the night, to flower, which should look amazing under the moon. Some of these plants attract night-time pollinators like huge moths and even flying foxes, and many of them are white or light colored so that the moonlight can reflect off them and they can be seen.

I can hear the chatter of the foxes tonight and the sweet voice of a small owl and, honestly, it would be easy to imagine I'm in an enchanted forest far away from any other human. The constant, though, is that big moon, making everything silver and full of glowing magic, and it is all there for me to weave with.

As I see more and more people every year discover the huge mental and physical benefits of working with the lunar cycles and seasonal energies it makes me more excited than ever to share a year with you with a magical companion such as this diary. This is our 14th edition (!), and I love how far we have come in evolving this diary to suit busy modern readers. However, most things I started with are still here. It was my strong intention from day one to provide good-quality, clear information so that you could get excited about working with the moon and the seasons and that you would be encouraged to take the information further in your life and in your workings. I wanted to show you through all the spells and suggestions that the moon doesn't work solo: it works with your energies and earthly energies such as the seasons, light, dark and other elements. This is an exciting aspect of the work to discover!

Again, you – yes, you – are not just part of the magic: you are the magic. You are the weaver. In fact, the root of the word 'witch' comes from the word 'weaver'. So you can feel the space in which to create your year I didn't want to give you rows of numbers and co-ordinates, but instead show you the way the moon and the seasons progress and work together, the way they invite you to join in with the flow.

I have structured this diary so you can connect deeply yet easily to the lunar and seasonal cycles and the wheel of the year, and of course there is a god or goddess of the month to guide and advise you. Each year I try to choose a mixture of well-known and lesser-known gods and goddesses for you to explore a connection with, and you get to try all kinds of witchcraft-based workings including invocations, meditations, rituals and spells.

You have told me that one of our newer features, a section at the beginning of each month to keep track of your ideas, action and intentions so you can flow forward with momentum throughout the year, is one of your favorite things about the diary. I personally think that having good structure actually gives us some freedom, so I'm super pleased about your engagement with this.

Whether you're a new practitioner or someone with vast experience, I look forward to the magic and power that I know you'll create this year.

Wishing you big magic

Stacey Demarco
THE MODERN WITCH

ABOUT SPELLCRAFT

How and why do spells work? This is a big question but it can be answered. For a detailed explanation check out the chapter that answers this in my book *There's a Witch in the Boardroom*, but the short answer is dependent on whether you wish to go the spiritual or scientific route . . . or both!

THE SPIRITUAL PATH

Witches and those from many other spiritual paths believe we are connected to all things, including the divine. The divine assists us in achieving our intentions when we communicate effectively what it is that we want or don't want. To perform spellcraft we need to clearly state what our intentions are and raise considerable energy around this intention before releasing it in a directed fashion. We then take steps towards what we need and desire and the divine meets us more than halfway. Magic happens; we get what we want.

THE SCIENTIFIC PATH

Spells speak the language of the subconscious, the part of the mind that directs us towards our goals and dreams. It's where ideas pop up from and where creativity is based. You can program the subconscious to focus on what you want through elements such as symbology, movement, visualisation and emotion, and spells are a great way to do this effectively.

Whichever explanation you prefer – or perhaps you prefer a little bit of both – know that spells, rituals and invocations work effectively.

FIVE TOP CASTING TIPS

1. Relax, have fun. One of the best ways to ensure powerful spellcraft is to leave all your administration tasks, worries and preconceived ideas behind and just let go. Spellcraft is meant to be a joyful practice. Even when you are casting to rid yourself of something you no longer need there is at least a feeling of satisfaction, calm or hope that things will now change for the better.

2. Don't worry if things don't go perfectly. So what if the candle blows out or the incense doesn't light or your phone rings: does that mean your spell is ruined? Well, only if you stop! Spells are more about knowing what you want and raising power behind this than whether or not things run perfectly. Be confident, hold your intention clearly and keep going!

3. Plan in advance. Sometimes a quickly planned spell is a good spell but, when you can, plan ahead, especially when it comes to timings. This diary gives you great timing information that you can use to pinpoint the best days to cast for your particular needs. Ensuring that you have any ingredients or supplies ahead of time will reduce your stress levels and leave you free to concentrate on your intentions.

I also think that it's important to plan for safety; for example, keeping children and animals away from flames and flames away from your animals and kids, using good-quality magical supplies (which you may have to order) and having the room well ventilated when using incense. Most important, though, is to plan by being crystal clear about what you are casting for. Your intention is of utmost importance, but if you don't know what you want then cast for clarity. Take time before starting to cast to examine what it is that you do or don't want and put this in clear concise language. After all, if you don't know what you want the universe can't co-create properly with you.

4. Don't interfere with free will. It is a terrible misconception that witchcraft is commonly used to directly control someone's mind or actions, but one of the key tenets of most witchcraft traditions is to never interfere with another person's free will. Spellcraft works very effectively, so it is not fair to impose your will or what you believe is the best thing for someone else upon another person. This means you shouldn't ever cast on or for other people, as it may have consequences. Even if someone is ill, I always ask permission before commencing any kind of healing invocation. If they are very ill and can't give permission I always add the direction '. . . if it be for the good of all' as a kind of insurance policy.

Love spells are probably the trickiest when it come to ensuring free will is intact. No matter what, never cast for a particular person; instead, cast for the kind of relationship and partner you desire. This means you will attract the best candidate – who may or may not be a person you know!

5. Participate! Equally important as having a clear intention is participating after the spell. This is a chance for you to get moving, choosing in the direction of your intention. After a spell is almost complete I always like to ask the divine for their suggestions on what to do next. The way this request is answered is rarely in a big booming voice that tells me clearly what to do. Instead, it comes as ideas do: effortlessly and easily, like just popping into my head. By actioning any or all of these messages you will be co-creating with the divine, which means you start moving. Even a small start has a ripple effect that will lead you to your intention more quickly.

SPELLCASTING MADE EASY

Everyone can cast! Everyone can write an effective spell if they follow the outlines in the spellcasting template below. Each spell has a skeleton, a structure that gives the spell form and function. Fill in this template and you will have the beginnings of a great spell, and remember to be creative and confident and have fun!

1. Focus
This is where you decide to cast a spell for a specific reason and begin to plan the process, taking into consideration time and ethics. This can include a list of things you'll need to cast the spell.

2. Purpose and intention
Clearly and concisely state what the spell is for and what you hope to manifest; for example, 'Great goddess, I am here to ask you to help me achieve [XYZ] quickly and easily' or 'Universe, I wish to attract my ideal partner for a committed relationship leading to marriage.'

3. Raising power
This is how you'll raise energy to boost your intention. Common ways are through raising your emotions or via meditation, drumming, dancing and moving.

4. Release
This is how you will release and send all the power you raised out in to the universe. It should be different from how you raised power; for example, burning something, clapping, shouting or suddenly stopping the movement.

5. Participation and grounding
This is the next step you'll take in the physical world to start manifesting what you want. You will often feel filled with energy after casting and may sometimes wish to ground that energy a little. Great ways to do this include having a bath or shower, placing your hands on the ground or on a plant or eating.

SPELL TIMINGS AND MOON CYCLES

One of the most common questions around spellcasting is: 'What is the best time to cast my spells?' The simple answer is *any time*. However, there are particular times that can be more powerful, and if you align yourself with them they can assist you in achieving greater success.

As we honor the earth and creation we closely observe the cycles of nature as our guide. These include the moon cycles, seasonal changes and the position of the sun in the sky. Traditionally, witches and pagans work closely with moon energy, which encompasses both the moon phases and the tides. This diary gives you clear information about moon phases and also offers suggestions about what to cast for. You can check tidal information with your local newspaper, weather channel or specialist website (see the Resources section at the end of this diary).

MOON PHASE TIMINGS 2024

DARK MOON	NEW MOON	FULL MOON
10 January	11 January, 6.57 am	25 January, 12.54 pm
8 February	9 February, 5.59 pm	24 February, 7.30 am
9 March	10 March, 5.00 am	25 March, 3.00 am
7 April	8 April, 2.20 pm	23 April, 7.48 pm
6 May	7 May, 11.21 pm	23 May, 9.53 am
5 June	6 June, 8.37 am	21 June, 9.07 pm
4 July	5 July, 6.57 pm	21 July, 6.17 am
3 August	4 August, 7.13 am	19 August, 2.25 pm
1 September	2 September, 9.55 pm	17 September, 10.34 pm
1 October	2 October, 2.49 pm	17 October, 7.26 am
31 October	1 November, 8.47 am	15 November, 4.28 pm
30 November	1 December, 1.21 am	15 December, 4.01 am
29 December	30 December, 5.26 pm	—

- All times are local times for New York, New York, USA.
- Time is adjusted for daylight savings time when applicable. Please adjust for your state/country.
- Dates are based on the Gregorian calendar.

SPECIAL MOON EVENTS IN 2024

- Super new moon: 9 February.
- Micro full moon: 24 February.
- Super new moon: 10 March.
- Penumbral lunar eclipse visible in New York: 25 March.
- Blue moon: 19 August.
- Super full moon: 17 September.
- Partial lunar eclipse visible in New York: 17–18 September.
- Micro new moon: 2 October.
- Super full moon: 17 October.
- Black moon: 30 December (usually each season has three months and three new moons; when a season has four new moons the third new moon is called a black moon).

WHAT THE MOON PHASES MEAN

Every moon is a magical moon! Below is some useful information on what each moon phase means for us in terms of energy, as well as some suggestions on what to cast and when.

FULL MOON

- The moon is full in the sky.
- Full energy! Big energy! Kapow!
- This moon gives you high-impact results and is perfect for attraction spells of any type.
- It's a great time to explore and find your true path and purpose in life.
- Witches formally celebrate their relationship with the divine once every 28 days during full moon. This is called an *esbat*; literally, a meeting with others in a coven or simply with the divine.

WANING MOON

- The moon is growing smaller in the sky. This occurs after a full moon and before a new moon.
- Energy is reduced.
- It's a good time to perform spells with a purpose and intention of getting rid of something that no longer serves you or to reduce an obstacle.
- It's a great time to give up a bad habit; for example, an addiction or a limiting or negative belief.

DARK MOON

- No moon is visible in the sky.
- Traditionally, this is a time of introversion and rest.
- It's a good time for spells that ask for peace and creative flow.
- Experienced witches can use this moon for powerful healing through positive hexing.

NEW MOON

- A new moon occurs the day after a dark moon and is good for fresh starts and renewal.
- Traditionally, it is the time to make seven wishes.
- It's a great time for casting spells to do with health and for the beginning of projects or businesses.
- It is a powerful time to cast spells for better mental health.

WAXING MOON

- The moon is growing larger in the sky. This happens after a new moon and before the full moon.
- Energy is growing and expanding.
- It's a good time to perform spells with a purpose and intention of growth and moving towards something you desire.
- It's a powerful time to ask for more money, more positive relationships and better health.
- It's a wonderful phase for prosperity spells.
- It's perfect for asking for bodily vitality, a pay rise, a new job or more recognition.

TIDES

Tides are, of course, linked to the moon. The rise and fall of the tides can be used as additional elements in your spells: aligning them with your spells make them even more powerful. Being by the sea or water and seeing the tides ebb and flow will always add an extra dimension to your spell or ritual.

HIGH TIDE

* High tides bring things towards you and are known for attraction.
* They are wonderful for prosperity spells.
* They are perfect for asking for better health, a pay rise, a new job or more recognition.

LOW TIDE

* Low tides remove things or takes things away.
* They are perfect for removing obstacles, negative feelings, pain, bad memories and office politics.

KING TIDE

* On super full moons the tides are very high and very low; these are king tides, and they happen on a regular basis.
* Use these opportunities well, as they are wonderful for calling in prosperity and business in particular.
* Energies during king tides are even more emphasized, so make sure what you ask for is what you truly desire. It may be worth holding a desire especially for a king tide if it is a request that can wait.

OTHER TIMINGS

DAWN

* New beginnings.
* New projects.
* Creativity spells.
* Initiations.

SUNSET

* Completions.
* Asking for help for a project or issue that may be long or difficult.
* Spells for faith and preparation.

Midday

- Asking for increased personal power.
- Asking for confidence and strength.
- Asking for the courage to allow your light to shine.
- Worshipping during fire festivals such as Litha.

Midnight

- The witching hour.
- Asking for self-knowledge.
- Asking for deep and lasting change.
- Asking for help from your ancestors.
- Turning dreams into reality.

Equinox and solstice timings: universal time (UTC)

- Spring equinox, Ostara, 20 March at 3.06 UTC.
- Summer solstice, Litha, 20 June at 20.50 UTC.
- Fall equinox, Mabon, 22 September at 12.43 UTC.
- Winter solstice, Yule, 21 December at 9.20 UTC.

Equinox and solstice timings: New York, New York, USA

- Spring equinox, Ostara, 19 March at 11.06 pm EDT*.
- Summer solstice, Litha, 20 June at 4.50 pm EDT*.
- Fall equinox, Mabon, 22 September at 8.43 am EDT**.
- Winter solstice, Yule, 21 December at 4.20 am EST*.

* Eastern daylight time: daylight savings adjusted.

** Eastern standard time.

ASTROLOGICAL CORRESPONDENCES
FOR KEY MOON PHASES 2024

MONTH	ASTROLOGICAL SIGN	NEW MOON	FULL MOON
January	Capricorn	11 January, 6.57 am	–
	Cancer	–	25 January, 12.54 pm
February	Aquarius	9 February, 5.59 pm	–
	Virgo	–	24 February, 7.30 am
March	Pisces	10 March, 5.00 am	–
	Libra	–	25 March, 3.00 am
April	Aries	8 April, 2.20 pm	–
	Libra	–	23 April, 7.48 pm
May	Taurus	7 May, 11.21 pm	–
	Scorpio	–	23 May, 9.53 am
June	Gemini	6 June, 8.37 am	–
	Capricorn	–	21 June, 9.07 pm
July	Cancer	5 July, 6.57 pm	–
	Capricorn	–	21 July, 6.17 am
August	Leo	4 August, 7.13 am	–
	Aquarius		19 August, 2.25 pm
September	Virgo	2 September, 9.55 pm	–
	Pisces	–	17 September, 10.34 pm
October	Libra	2 October, 2.49 pm	–
	Aries	–	17 October, 7.26 am
November	Scorpio	1 November, 8.47 am	–
	Taurus	–	15 November, 4.28 pm
December	Sagittarius	1 December, 1.21 am	–
	Gemini	–	15 December, 4.01 am
	Capricorn	30 December, 5.26 pm	–

WHAT DO THE ASTROLOGICAL SIGNS MEAN?

Separate to the meanings of the phases of the moon and the timings of the wheel of the year, there is also the layer of meaning often added where the moon is transiting within the signs of the zodiac. The moon makes a full transit of the earth (and the signs) every two and a half days.

I have listed below the astrological phases of the moon and some corresponding themes around which magical workings can be performed extra effectively. When the moon is in:

CAPRICORN

Excellent for magic concerning planning, clarity, strategy, career, purpose, status and obstacle busting.

AQUARIUS

Excellent for magic concerning popularity, strengthening friendships, change, creativity, science, deepening spirituality and for the greater good.

PISCES

Great timing for magical workings concerning dreams, completion, increasing psychic ability and intuition and flow and also a good time to do healing work around women's cycles.

ARIES

Great timing for magical workings concerning stamina, leadership, dealing with authority figures, strength and study.

TAURUS

Excellent for magic concerning family and children, love, home matters, the purchase of real estate and creating sacred space in the home.

GEMINI

Great timing for magic concerning expansion, communication of all kinds, travel, writing and invocations.

CANCER

Great timing for magical workings concerning all kinds of emotional healing, cutting cords of old relationships, healing the body and promoting health, particularly through diet.

LEO

Excellent for magical workings concerning self-esteem, personal power, status, authority of all kinds and improving your relationship with your boss.

VIRGO

Great timing for magical workings concerning getting or keeping a job, exams, purification, clearing and detoxing of all kinds.

LIBRA

Excellent timing for magical workings concerning balance, justice, all legal matters, better health and weight balance.

SCORPIO

Great timing for magical workings concerning all sexual matters, healing trauma, reducing gossip and increasing fun.

SAGITTARIUS

Excellent timing for magical workings concerning truth, exposing dishonesty, clarity and to ask for increased travel or protection during travel.

ELEMENTS AND DIRECTIONS

You might wish to utilize the elements and directions in your spells and workings to give yet another layer of powerful symbology and energy. Experienced witches use a compass (cell phones generally have one) if they are not sure of the directions when setting up a circle.

Below are some suggestions for ways of honoring each direction and corresponding element, but ultimately the combinations are up to you and certainly the geography around you. It used to be that there were very strict correspondences, usually highly influenced by the northern hemisphere, but now pagans and witches all over the world combine the elements and directions in the way that the geography in front of them most calls for. So, for example, if you were standing facing east in Sydney, Australia the dominant element in the environment would be the ocean (water); thus I cast east as water.

EARTH – NORTH

- Salt, earth and oils such as oak moss and patchouli.
- Standing on earth, sprinkling earth and salt, anointing stones.
- Represents resilience, order, law, politics, education, security and money.
- Green/brown.
- Night.

FIRE – SOUTH

- Candles, open flame of any kind and oils such as pepper, ginger and frankincense.
- Lighting a flame, passing a flame around the circle and anointing with oil.
- Represents passion, purpose, strength, achievement and the destruction of what is not needed.
- Masculine: sun.
- Red.
- Noon.

AIR – EAST

- Incense, fragrance, smoke, kites, balloons and oils such as bergamot, lime and eucalyptus.
- Smudging, blowing smoke, bubbles, bells and singing bowls.
- Represents communication, creativity, logic, travel, new beginnings, ideas and flow.
- Yellow.
- Dawn.

WATER – WEST

- Salt water, moon water, shells, rain and oils such as rose and ylang ylang.
- Anointing with water and passing the cup.
- Relationships, love, psychic connection and birth/death/rebirth.
- Represents relationships, love, psychic connection and birth/death/rebirth.
- Feminine: moon.
- Blue.

WHEEL OF THE YEAR

As the path of the witch is an earth-based faith the witches' sabbats, or holidays, are intrinsically connected with the cycles of nature. Primarily, the themes of birth, death and rebirth are played out across a year that is divided into light and dark, male and female, sun and moon, growth and rest and heat and cold.

Traditionally, most of the celebrations were linked to the cycles of the northern hemisphere, which became confusing for witches in the southern hemisphere. Should southern hemisphere witches follow the traditional wheel of the year timings even though they are opposite to their seasons, or should they adapt and reverse the wheel so it is in rhythm with their environment?

Like most witches in the southern hemisphere I follow the wheel so that it more closely fits my unique natural seasonal cycles, and for this diary I have aligned the celebrations along these dates.

Importantly, these sacred times connect you with the light, land and seasons. The land is our mother: she feeds us, shelters us and gives us comfort and joy. The festivals give us a chance to give something back to her and honor all that she does. As modern people we often forget this and feel disconnected without quite knowing why.

The continuous cycle lends itself to the image of a wheel, as you can see. The ancient Celts and their predecessors saw time as a wheel or spiral divided by eight festivals, as listed below. Modern witches can use the themes of each celebration to do magical workings of their own in complete synergy with the natural cycles. The dates featured on solstices and equinoxes should be used as a guide only, so please refer to the diary itself for accuracy.

NOTE: where these festivals fall within the calendar spreads within this diary I have given further information on the festival and some suggestions on how to celebrate the Sabbath with meaning.

SAMHAIN (HALLOWE'EN)

- Southern hemisphere 30 April; northern hemisphere 31 October.
- Celebration of death as a continuation of life.
- Borders between the dead and living are not fixed and impassable.
- The veil between the worlds is at it thinnest, so you can ask the ancestors and spirits for guidance on and communication about the future.
- Celebrating where you came from; ancestral energy.
- Traditional time for scrying.
- Witches' New Year!

YULE (WINTER SOLSTICE)

- Southern hemisphere 21–23 June; northern hemisphere 21–23 December.
- Longest night of the year.
- Mid-winter festival linked to the Christian Christmas.
- Archetypally linked with the birth of a child of promise and light: Dionysus, Arthur, Jesus, Baldur.
- Celebrates the return of the sun and thus hope.
- Abundance spells and charms.
- Giving thanks and gifts of goodwill.

IMBOLC (CANDLEMAS)

- Southern hemisphere 1 August; northern hemisphere 1 February.
- Celebration of light returning.
- Goddess as Brigid (St Brigid).
- Fire festival.
- Clarity and healing.
- Shine your light, self-knowledge/creation.

OSTARA (SPRING EQUINOX)

- Southern hemisphere 21–23 September; northern hemisphere 21–23 March.
- Night and day are equal but moving towards the long days of summer.
- Balance and growth.
- Leave what you don't want and create the new things.
- Fertility and love.
- Fresh projects.

BELTANE (MAY DAY)

- Southern hemisphere 31 October; northern hemisphere 30 April–1 May.
- Marriage of the goddess and the god.
- May pole: phallic and yonic symbolism.
- Love magic and fertility: weddings and handfastings.
- Masculine and feminine balances.

LITHA (SUMMER SOLSTICE)

- Southern hemisphere 21–23 December; northern hemisphere 21–23 June.
- Longest day and the shortest night.
- The sun is at its fullest power although the year begins to wane from now.
- Uncover what brings light and joy into your life and develop this.
- Self-development.
- Celebration of the masculine divine.

LAMMAS (LUGHNASADH)

- Southern hemisphere 1 February; northern hemisphere 1 August.
- First harvest; the first loaf is baked.
- The god begins his journey into the underworld.
- Sorrow and celebration.
- Fruition and taking stock and harvesting what you have achieved.

MABON (AUTUMN EQUINOX)

- Southern hemisphere 21–22 March; northern hemisphere 21–22 September.
- Harvesting the main crop.
- Take stock of what has served you well and what has not.
- What needs repairing before the dark comes.
- Preparation for harder times.
- Welcoming change energy.

THE MOON AND OUR BODY

We are moon-influenced animals, even if most of us don't go howling under it! Within long-held knowledge there are a number of ways that it's believed the moon impacts our physical bodies.

HAIR

I know many of you lunar-tics love cutting and growing your hair by the moon's cycles, and I know that full and new moon days are some of the most popular days for hairdressers all over the world. It is thought that different phases influence hair growth just as they influence tides, so it's no surprise that full and waxing moons are best friends to those of us who want longer locks!

Growing your hair: traditionally, should you wish to grow your hair only cut it when it is in its most active phase during a full or waxing moon.

Keeping your hair a similar length: if you wish to preserve your haircut (very handy for those who have a fringe or short hair), cut your hair on a waning moon.

Strengthening your hair: for hair treatment days you might try new moon days and waxing moons. For the mother of all good hair days go for the full moon in Cancer for all your conditioning and cutting treatments.

For hair removal: whether you wax, laser or shave, the best time to take hair off is in a waning moon cycle as it will stay away longer.

WEIGHT BALANCE

In ethical witchcraft we don't talk about losing weight. Instead, it's about having the body reach a healthy balance. Setting your intention and beginning on a full moon is a great idea, as it gets your mind used to the idea that this is a great idea and is something you want. You might even cast a spell for health and vitality that night to boost it along; there is a good one free on my site www.themodernwitch.com.

Waning moon: begin your program straight after a full moon and notice that the moon is waning and thus taking with it extra weight and fluid. You will lose more weight more rapidly during a waning moon if this is what you seek.

New moon: when the moon reaches a new phase do another ritual to boost your intention. Lighting a candle and simply asking the universe to continue to assist you to reach your goal and to achieve greater health is enough.

Waxing moon: you must be careful during this phase not to eat foods that are not aligned with your intention, as waxing moon cycles will hold them to your body far more than during waning cycles. However, you will generally have more energy during waxing moon phases so this is the time to boost your activity levels and more easily burn off what you consume.

Back to full moon: be grateful for what you have achieved or achieved so far and set your intention moving forward. Express love and admiration for what your body is and does.

BALANCING YOUR BODY WITH THE MOON

There is some excellent research available on the correlation of lunar light, moon phase and bodily biorhythms like those related to hormonal and fertility cycles. There seems to be two camps on this: in the first there seems to be no correlation with the moon cycles of 28 to 29 days with the typical female cycle of the same length or with a spike in fertility around the full moon, while the second camp recognizes this long-held wisdom as fact.

If you're female and have a menstrual cycle that is radically less than or more than 29 days you may consider it beneficial to balance your cycle. One way that seems to work is to literally watch the moon for five minutes each night. We need light to activate a whole cascade of bodily functions, and it seems the fertility cycle is but one of them. If you wish you could visualize your most fertile time at a full moon (full power!) and your wise blood flowing around a dark/new moon (letting go, starting afresh).

THE LUNAR RETURN

Across a number of ancient cultures such as the Egyptian and Sumerian it was believed that the moon phase at birth triggered the beginning of life and remained as a person's energetic peak time throughout life. This was especially evident for women, as it determined their most fertile time. Records of Sumerian medicine indicated a belief that a woman was most fertile when the moon was at the same phase as her birth. Ancient Celts and Egyptians recorded the moon phase at birth and told both sexes when they came of age. This is known as a 'lunar return'.

A lunar return is not what astrological moon sign you were born in; it's more astronomy than astrology. Rather, it's what actual phase was in the sky when you were born; for example, a full moon, quarter moon, two days before a new moon and so on.

The simple idea of knowing which phase of the moon you were born during and noting it as well as keeping an eye on the moon regularly seems to induce more hormonal balance in both sexes. It is also the peak time of performance for mental and physical energy. Knowing when you will be feeling most vital and energetic really does have profound impacts in everyday life, as does knowing when you are at the top of your game for sport, exams or decision-making. Knowing when you may not have a lot of energy (the opposite of your lunar return moon) is also valuable to know.

DEITIES OF THE MOON

One of the aspects of lunar lore that I fell in love with pretty quickly as a young person was that of the gods and goddesses. I loved mythos – the stories with a truth – even as a child, and as I grew I began to understand that these stories and art weren't just little fairy tales such as the one about the man on the moon but were instead so much deeper and more instructive. The deities could help me transform myself and flow forward just as the moon phases did. These amazing queens, goddesses, gods and kings led by example and, boy, don't we all need good strong examples?

Witches believe that we each have a spark of the goddess and god within us and, in natural reciprocity, the goddess and god have a spark of us within them. Knowing intimately that if you have a spark of divinity within you are indeed a goddess or god tends to change reality for you. It is difficult to experience self-hate if you know that you have the divine within you: self-esteem comes flowing back, flooding you with positive change if you truly come to this realisation.

Below are some deities I recommend to work with who have links with the moon.

Artemis (Greek)

Aradia (Roman)

Arianrhod (Welsh)

Brigid (Celtic)

Cerridwen (Welsh)

Circe (Greek)

Diana (Roman)

Freyja (Norse)

Hina (Polynesian)

Hekate (Greek)

Mani (Norse)

Morgan le Fay (Celtic)

Skadi (Norse)

Thoth (Egyptian)

Triple Goddess (archetype, European wiccan)

Yemaya (Yoruban)

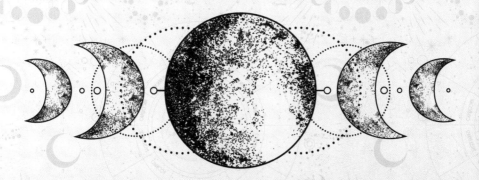

LUNAR ENERGIES
AND CRYSTALS

✳

Utilizing crystals to focus and capture energy is something that many pagan and non-pagan practitioners do. One of the most popular ways of cleansing and charging your crystals is to place them under the moonlight. However, there are some subtle ways of enhancing the energies of crystals by matching the specific lunar energy at certain times in the cycle or by using solar energy instead.

LUNAR ENERGIES

Cleansing: leave your crystals out under the power of a full or waxing moon. If you are using the powers of a waxing moon, leave the crystals out on multiple nights right up to the full moon.

Dedicating for matters of prosperity: I have had success with leaving crystals out in the moonlight in a bowl of shallow water. The water promotes the flow of money towards you.

Dedicating for matters of growth: place your crystals on living soil or a plant. Grass is perfect, as is a healthy pot plant. Leave the crystals under moonlight and then for a full day of sunshine as well.

Dedicating to absorb negative energies: many crystals are useful in the way they help dispel or absorb negative energies; jet, obsidian, black tourmaline and pink kunzite are good examples of this. Give these crystals an extra boost by dedicating them or charging them on a dark or waning moon cycle.

Dedicating for meditation or channeling: I very much like to dedicate stones such as lapis lazuli, amethyst, clear quartz or turquoise during dark moon phases when the energies are aligned for more introverted, inward-facing activities. I like to take these crystals into the darker parts of my garden or even areas shaded slightly by rocks but still able to be graced by the sky. I try and retrieve them just before dawn to keep the integrity of the darkness intact.

SOLAR ENERGIES

While I love to leave my crystals out basking in the silvery moonlight, there are some crystals that thrive under a fiery sun. I find that naturally gold- or warm-coloured stones such as amber and citrine often need a good dose of solar energy to keep them happy, so don't be afraid to leave them under a blazing sun. When dedicating your crystals you will still need to cleanse them first in whichever manner works best for you, but here are some charging and dedication suggestions using solar energies that work for me.

Dedicating for health: on three days running from dawn until dusk, leave out those crystals that will be dedicated to health and healing. Midsummer is an ideal time to do this, as is the time around a new moon.

Dedicating for inspiration: get a boost from the biggest fire of all to fan your personal fires of inspiration – the sun. Place your stones on a natural surface such as grass or a plant and leave them out from dawn until dusk for seven days. Springtime is a great time to do this each year.

Gifts: when I'm giving a crystal to a man I always leave it out under the sun for a day or so. The sun gives the stone a charging of masculine energy, which I believe enables it to bind more quickly to its new owner. For women, leave the crystal under the moon.

CRYSTALS FOR MOON PHASES

Below is a list of the crystals I find really compatible and powerful with particular moon phases. You can use them in gridding or mandala, on your altar, to boost spells and energy raising or wear them, carry them or pop them in a juju bag. The stones I believe are great universals with lunar energy are clear quartz, Herkimer diamonds and diamonds. You can also try metals such as platinum and silver, and as pearls are from the ocean they are also very compatible with lunar workings.

Dark moon: jet

New moon: celestine

Waxing crescent 1: aventurine

Waxing crescent 2: lepidolite

Waxing crescent 3: charoite

Waxing crescent 4: rose quartz

Waxing crescent 5: emerald

Waxing crescent 6: pyrite

First quarter moon: azurite

Waxing gibbous 1: yellow jasper

Waxing gibbous 2: aquamarine

Waxing gibbous 3: obsidian

Waxing gibbous 4: hematite

Waxing gibbous 5: carnelian

Waxing gibbous 6: rhodonite

Full moon: moonstone

Waning gibbous 1: tiger's eye

Waning gibbous 2: turquoise

Waning gibbous 3: bloodstone

Waning gibbous 4: larimar

Waning gibbous 5: azurite

Waning gibbous 6: fluorite

Last quarter moon: ocean jasper

Waning crescent 1: black tourmaline

Waning crescent 2: red jasper

Waning crescent 3: orange calcite

Waning crescent 4: smokey quartz

Waning crescent 5: amethyst

THE MOON AND PLANTS

For millennia, people all over the planet have been farming and gardening by the moon's cycles. It is believed that because earth operates under a gravity field that is influenced by the moon this affects the growth of plants. It is believed that the moon changes the level of water in the soil, which affects seedling and plant growth.

There are amazing farmer's almanacs you can buy for your region each year that give very detailed planting suggestions and harvesting recommendations, all guided by the moon and astrological information (see the Resources section). While this isn't a gardening diary, I have added some suggestions and it certainly is worth mentioning here the basic lunar rules of thumb when it comes to gardening by the moon. Knowing how the moon can influence your patch may make the difference between a fair, good or bumper crop.

FULL MOON

As the water rises and swells within the soil it's the perfect time to plant seeds. It is also a good time to harvest some plants at the peak of their goodness.

WANING MOON

As the water level sinks during a waning moon phase it's time to plant below-ground plants such as potatoes, carrots, onions, parsnips and beetroot.

NEW MOON

During a new moon phase growth slows, so it's time to prune, trim, fertilize and weed and apply any necessary natural pest control.

WAXING MOON

A waxing moon phases is growth time again and water begins to rise. It's a good time to plant above-ground crops such as pumpkin, tomatoes, cauliflower, kale, lettuce and spinach.

FERTILE ZODIAC SIGNS

Water and earth signs are considered the growth times for plants. When the moon enters these signs it's a fine time to plant or prune back for growth.

BARREN ZODIAC SIGNS

All your maintenance chores should be done on the times when the moon is in fire and air signs.

You can learn more in my book *The Enchanted Moon*.

STARTING YOUR
YEAR POSITIVELY

This section is about learning how to ask for and get what you really want.

There are a lot of people who have decided they won't even attempt new year resolutions anymore because they can never keep them. Yes, we know that some people set unreasonable goals (lose huge amounts of weight in one month anyone?), but it seems that the big reason we don't achieve what we say we want to achieve is that, really, we don't want it all that badly.

'I do want it, though!' you might say. 'I really do want to get healthy' or 'I really do want that new car/house/job/love!' Here is the big reason why you may not want it all that much: because right now it either doesn't align with your values or you have goals that actually belong to someone else. You simply aren't that devoted or you get distracted. Then for some there is the fear that if you get what you desire, what then: will your family still love you? Will the new job actually be really better? Will your life change so much you can't control it anymore?

Take all of those fears and look at them and feel them. That smells like confusion to me!

What I have done to assist you to get clearer about what you really want is an exercise I get participants in my infamous new year workshops to do (see later in this diary). If you fill this out before you do any new year spells or rituals I think you may find you get a big truth bomb hitting you in a very good way. You'll sort out what matters to you – really – and you can base your resolutions on that and be devoted to what you want to be rather than what you might be unconsciously doing. You will be able to track your progress and update it as you grow each month on the month header pages.

For me, I love the gateway of the new year because it is certainly a gateway into a fresh start if I wish it to be. It's a kind of catalyst for change. Many ancient cultures saw the beginning of a new year as an opportunity to journey through a gateway into something new, although to do so meant a leap of faith both literally and figuratively.

The Romans, for example, took this idea literally, creating new year doorways dedicated to the goddess Jana and the god Janus through which people jumped to signify that they had indeed left the energy of the previous year behind and fully accepted a new start. The Mayans smashed statues within gateways that represented the old year when that one was up and then walked over the rubble to get to the new year gateway.

Yes, we can all jump through a new gateway. We can all be brave and courageous and inspired. We can all be the leaders and heroes and happy endings in own story. So let us begin . . .

GETTING CLEAR
ABOUT 2024

Here are some great questions to ask yourself to get clear about what you want for 2024.

- **What are my values?** (Values are guiding ideals and principles; for example, honesty, compassion, creativity, calmness, fairness, independence, freedom.)

  _____

- **What are my needs?** (Needs are things you must have to be at your best.)

  _____

- **What am I devoted to right now?** (You can be devoted to things that are positive or not so positive and are devoted to what you actually do; for example, if you eat a lot of potato chips then you are devoted to eating potato chips.)

  _____

- **What do I want to be devoted to?**

  _____

- **Take those values and needs and think about what would give you the greatest pleasure in 2024.**

  _____

Get even clearer by discerning further based on your values and real pleasures.

- **What would I definitely wish to leave behind in 2023?** (For example, think about old patterns, negative experiences, bad habits, ill health and so on.)

  _____

- **Based on my values and pleasures, what would I love to experience but haven't as yet?**

  _____

- If I could make one positive intention for the community or planet as a whole it would be:

_____

- Taking all this into consideration, the new year intentions I would love to set are:

_____

- The steps I will take for each month of 2024 are:

January: _____

February: _____

March: _____

April: _____

May: _____

June: _____

July: _____

August: _____

September: _____

October: _____

November: _____

December: _____

NEW YEAR'S GATEWAY JUMP

As did the ancient Romans, I love a good new year's gateway jump! Every year I start the year this way, and I know many of you have now gotten on board with this ritual and do it every year too. The ancient Romans obviously enjoyed this leaping through the gateway of the new year with the goddess Jana and god Janus, who face backwards and forwards at the same time. This is a fun ritual to do alone or with friends and there are lots of versions of it, although all of them involve a physical jump. I think this also kick-starts our mind and spirit.

GATEWAY RITUAL

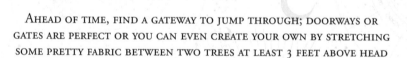

AHEAD OF TIME, FIND A GATEWAY TO JUMP THROUGH; DOORWAYS OR GATES ARE PERFECT OR YOU CAN EVEN CREATE YOUR OWN BY STRETCHING SOME PRETTY FABRIC BETWEEN TWO TREES AT LEAST 3 FEET ABOVE HEAD LEVEL OR PLACING A BROOM ON THE FLOOR AND LEAPING OVER IT.

Gather together: some incense to burn • a gift for the genus loci (the friendly spirits of the place) • a piece of chalk or a ribbon or broom to mark the gateway jump • a silver candle • a gold candle • a bowl of water with two handfuls of salt added • your list of intentions for the new year of 2024.

Go to where you are going to do the jump. Burn the incense in a bowl and allow the smoke to purify the area. You might thank the genus loci of the place for their help and leave a little gift.

When you are done, draw a line with the chalk or place the ribbon across the ground of the threshold of the gateway or doorway.

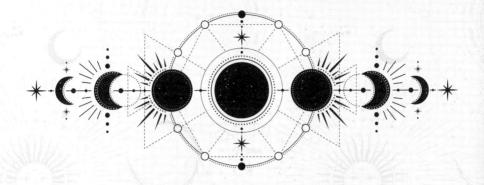

LIGHT THE SILVER CANDLE AND SAY:

'Jana of the gateway, goddess of what was and what will be! I am ready to step though 2023 into the sparkling new possibility of 2024. I have thought about my desires and wish you to grant my intentions if they be for the good of all!'

LIGHT THE GOLD CANDLE AND SAY:

'Janus of the gateway, you are the god of what is behind me and what is in front of me! I am ready to leap excitely into the future of 2024. Help me achieve my intentions and so much more if it be for the good of all!'

PLACE YOUR HANDS IN THE BOWL OF SALTED WATER AND SAY:

'In your presence I clear away any burdens or poor actions. I cleanse away my fears, doubts and any obstacles in the way of this, a new year!'

Wash your hands, imagining all negative things in your life being cleansed, then read out your intentions for 2024 three times.

Be excited about these intentions: don't be shy about them! Feel that excitement ripple right through your body.

STEP TOWARDS THE GATEWAY OR THRESHOLD AND SAY IN A CLEAR VOICE:

'Jana and Janus, take me through the gateway easily and with your protection. I step forward into the new!'

STEP OR JUMP CONFIDENTLY FORWARD THROUGH THE GATEWAY AND SAY:

'Thank you! Yes!'

CLAP LOUDLY THREE TIMES. THANK JANA AND JANUS AND ASK:

'What do I do next?'

Listen for any messages or ideas and act upon these as soon as you can.

Blow out the candles after midnight if possible and throw the salted water down the drain.

Happy New Year, fellow jumpers!

JANUARY

◆ What would I like to create, experience and manifest this month?

_____

_____

_____

_____

◆ What are the important dates for me this month?

_____

_____

◆ What would give me joy this month?

_____

_____

◆ What am I devoted to?

_____

_____

◆ Ideas, musings and actions:

_____

_____

_____

BOREAS

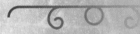

In the ancient Greek world there were deities of the elements and they were significant, especially in early Greece. Wind, being an important element, had four seasonal gods called *Anemoi*. The biting north wind was represented by the god Boreas.

Boreas, who was also considered to be the god of winter, swept down from Mount Haemus in Thrace bringing ice, snow and cold with him. He is said, nevertheless, to be a comely god, swiftly moving and having deep purple wings. In art he is often depicted as a powerful man in the prime of his life with a beard with icicles or blowing wind from his mouth. His wife was Oreithyia ('mountain gale'), his daughter was Khione, the goddess of snow, and his sons were the Boreades, winged heroes who did beneficial things.

The Greeks considered Boreas to be an entity who was able to breathe his incredible power into others, and certainly this energy was part of the siring of the 12 immortal horses of the kings of Troy. The Hippoi Troiades were the swiftest and most beautiful horses on earth and were the children of Boreas. They were gifted to King Laomedon by Zeus as compensation for the theft of Ganymedes.

Later the hero Herakles was promised the horses as a reward by Laomedon for rescuing his daughter Hesione from a great sea monster. After rescuing the princess,

Herakles went to claim his horses but Laomedon reneged. A bitter siege resulted and Laomedon lost his kingdom and his horses.

You didn't need to be a king in Greece to benefit from Boreas' power with horses. It is said all mares could be blessed by impregnation by the winter wind and sometimes you could see the wind itself form into wild stallions. This power and speed meant that these horses of Greece were renowned the ancient world over.

SPELL FOR POWER

WE ALL NEED TO STRENGTHEN OUR PERSONAL POWER AT SOME STAGE, SO TRY THIS WORKING TO DO SO. THIS SPELL IS BEST DONE ON A WINDY DAY, AND THE COLDER THE BETTER.

Gather together: a small amount of wine in a glass ⬩ a length of silver or blue ribbon around 3 feet in length and wide enough to write on ⬩ a felt-tipped pen ⬩ a tree or large bush.

Take a breath, and close your eyes if you like.
If it's windy, allow the wind to flow around you.

SAY:

*'It is here that it begins. I call upon you, elder god Boreas,
king of the north and creator of the fastest horses.'*

POUR THE WINE UPON THE EARTH AND SAY:

'Please accept my offering.'

Write on the ribbon with the felt-tipped pen where it is you need more power in your life: perhaps it's more courage, more influence at work or more power in your creative endeavors (choose no more than three).

LOOSELY TIE ONE END OF THE RIBBON TO THE TREE OR BUSH SO YOU DON'T DAMAGE THE TREE, KNOT IT THREE TIMES AND SAY:

'Grant me power in these ways, as you catch my requests.'

Let the wind catch the ribbon and
send your wishes to Boreas.

1 Monday

Waning

New Year's Eve spell: set your intentions for 2024 now if you haven't previously. Cast the spell with Jana and Janus of the gateway or mark the end of this year with a small ritual of gratitude before you go out to celebrate. Just a simple candle lit with intention and a special honoring of all the energies or deities that assisted you this year is a great start.

Welcome to a new year!

Catch the wave of global fresh start, new beginnings energy. Cast BIG magic!

2 Tuesday

Waning

3 Wednesday

Waning

4 Thursday

Waning

5 Friday

Waning

Friday was named after Freyja, the Norse goddess of love, war and magic.

6 Saturday

Waning

7 Sunday

Waning

The dark to the full
Ride the cycle.

- THE GODDESS

JANUARY

M	T	W	T	F	S	S
1	**2**	**3**	**4**	**5**	**6**	**7**
8	9	10	11	12	13	14
15	16	17	18	19	20	21
22	23	24	25	26	27	28
29	30	31				

JANUARY

8 Monday

Waning

9 Tuesday

Waning

10 Wednesday

Dark moon

Relax into the first dark moon of the year and let go of what you do not need.

11 Thursday ☽ New moon in Capricorn 6.57 am EST

This new moon invites clean, clear, fresh starts. Set intentions for new beginnings large and small.

12 Friday

Waxing

13 Saturday

Waxing

14 Sunday

Waxing

JANUARY

M	T	W	T	F	S	S
1	2	3	4	5	6	7
8	**9**	**10**	**11**	**12**	**13**	**14**
15	16	17	18	19	20	21
22	23	24	25	26	27	28
29	30	31				

15 Monday ☽

Waxing

16 Tuesday ☽

Waxing

17 Wednesday ☽

Waxing

18 Thursday ☽

Waxing

19 Friday

Waxing

20 Saturday

Waxing

21 Sunday

Waxing

JANUARY

M	T	W	T	F	S	S
1	2	3	4	5	6	7
8	9	10	11	12	13	14
15	**16**	**17**	**18**	**19**	**20**	**21**
22	23	24	25	26	27	28
29	30	31				

22 Monday

Waxing

23 Tuesday

Waxing

24 Wednesday

Waxing

25 Thursday ◯ Full moon in Cancer 12.54 pm EST

This is a time to be scrupulous with the truth under a moon that is good for casting for emotional balance and illumination.

26 Friday ◑

Waning

27 Saturday ◑

Waning

28 Sunday ◑

Waning

A world within a seed.

- THE GODDESS.

JANUARY
M T W T F S S

M	T	W	T	F	S	S
1	2	3	4	5	6	7
8	9	10	11	12	13	14
15	16	17	18	19	20	21
22	**23**	**24**	**25**	**26**	**27**	**28**
29	30	31				

FEBRUARY

◆ What would I like to create, experience and manifest this month?

_____

_____

_____

_____

◆ What are the important dates for me this month?

_____

_____

_____

◆ What would give me joy this month?

_____

_____

_____

◆ What am I devoted to?

_____

_____

_____

◆ Ideas, musings and actions:

_____

_____

_____

LAKA

GODDESS OF THE MONTH: FEBRUARY

One of the most beautiful and ancient dances I have ever seen is that of the native Hawaiians, the hula. Hula is often misunderstood as some dance performed just for tourists, but it is far from that.

Laka is the goddess of hula. The root of the word *laka* means to be 'gentle' or 'magnetic in attraction'. Laka is a goddess of the green forest and the showers of rain that nourish it. She is the wife of Lono, the god of peace and fertility.

Hula is a complex art. A visual prayer to the gods and goddesses, it is a way to pass on stories and culture to the community and all generations past and present and future. Even though hula looks graceful, elegant and almost weightless it is an incredibly physical dance. It is performed by women and men and is as inspirational to watch as it is to dance.

Traditionally before commencing a hula the dancer asks to be inspired by and embody Laka. The feeling of complete inspiration, *ho'oulu*, is a kind of surrender to the power of the goddess and a willingness to be moved by her. The highest form of dancing is that which is inspired by Laka.

Should you wish to see the true art and glory of hula I suggest you watch the annual Merry Monarch Festival held in Hawaii. Here hula is elevated as it should be, and dancers come from all over Polynesia to perform and compete. We are lucky to be able to experience hula, as it was a part of the Hawaiian culture that was not encouraged by missionaries and colonists.

Allow Laka's graceful power to inspire you.

Ritual for inspiration

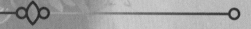

This spell should ideally be cast at a new moon phase, but every moon on a waxing cycle is also good. It should also be done outdoors if possible and with bare feet.

Gather together: a green candle; matches • a bright flower as an offering • a second bright flower for your hair.

Light the candle. Hold the bright flower in your hand and offer it to Laka.

Say out loud:

'Goddess Laka, bless me with your ho'oulu, your flow of inspiration.'

State out loud exactly where you need inspiration to flow: is it in creative work, in love or in business or in all of those things?

Hold the second flower, close your eyes and pull up energy from the earth. As you breathe in, take in love from the whole planet. Allow yourself to experience the emotion clearly and allow it to spread into every cell. Take your time. Bend your knees slightly and feel the earth strongly underneath your feet.

Place the flower in your hair or behind your ear; this is the blessing from Laka. Allow yourself to sway from side to side, again feeling the energy and inspiration of Laka.

Say thank you and know that Laka will assist you going forward.

Blow out the candle.

WHEEL OF THE YEAR

Imbolc

I think you feel spring even before you see it because there is an energetic awakening, a sacred shake, an awareness that things are moving again. Imbolc is the epitome of that earthly stretch after a sleep, the first real indication that the light and warmth are with us again and the transition between winter and spring is indeed happening.

Imbolc allows us to celebrate the returning of the light after the darkness of winter. It is an ancient Celtic festival that has as its origins a spring celebration honoring the goddess Brigid in her fire aspect. The Celts celebrated her fire sparking again and awakening the earth. On Imbolc morning Brigid walked the land and spread the warmth of her fertility and creative fire, bringing life back to the land.

Every Imbolc you can choose to awaken from anything that is heavy or empty, emerging from your winter cocoon and changing your focus if you need to. You can see where a new beginning would benefit you. You can also take this seasonal transition as a reminder to align yourself with the warmer time by changing your diet, spring cleaning (metaphorically and physically) and getting outside more. This is also a fantastic time of year to create talismans for growth and fertility.

HOW TO CELEBRATE IMBOLC

I start preparing for Imbolc a few days beforehand by cleaning and blessing my house and altar. I prepare fragrant flower waters of rose and mint and sprinkle this on my altar and desk, and I also wash floors, windows and statues with the water.

A spring altar is beautiful and easy to create and should be a feast for the senses. Cakes, flowers and loose petals are features on my altar, and I also light fragrant candles. I may make a few traditional Brigid's crosses out of straw (there are many videos on the internet that will show you how to make these).

Then, of course, we have the most fun and wonderful way to celebrate the coming of spring and Brigid: the blessing of the waters on Imbolc morning. As Brigid is the bringer of fire as well as being the goddess of water sources such as wells, we know it is she who can transform water into something sacred.

On Imbolc eve just as the sun sets, leave out an offering for Brigid. I like to leave out cream, milk, honey or cakes along with a bowl of water. It is said Brigid will bless the water, the very essence of regeneration and rebirth. You can drink the water for health and vitality or bathe in some, or as the old stories go rub some on your face and you won't age another year!

29 Monday

Waning

How are those new year intentions going?

30 Tuesday

Waning

31 Wednesday

Waning

May Brigid's blessings be upon you. Tomorrow is the festival of Imbolc; leave out a bowl of water for Brigid to bless for your health and beauty.

1 Thursday

Waning

Imbolc: the joyful festival of the return of the light! May the blessings of Brigid be upon you.

2 Friday 🌗

Waning

3 Saturday 🌗

Waning

4 Sunday 🌗

Waning

Hold your sacred boundary of self strongly.

– THE GODDESS

JANUARY								FEBRUARY						
M	**T**	**W**	**T**	**F**	**S**	**S**		**M**	**T**	**W**	**T**	**F**	**S**	**S**
1	2	3	4	5	6	7					**1**	**2**	**3**	**4**
8	9	10	11	12	13	14		5	6	7	8	9	10	11
15	16	17	18	19	20	21		12	13	14	15	16	17	18
22	23	24	25	26	27	28		19	20	21	22	23	24	25
29	**30**	**31**						26	27	28	29			

5 Monday

Waning

6 Tuesday

Waning

7 Wednesday

Waning

8 Thursday

Dark moon

Clear the decks and rest and rejuvenate. Let go of what you do not need.

9 Friday 🌙 New moon in Aquarius 5.59 pm EST

Super new moon

This powerful and inventive new moon is perfect to begin visionary projects or to action fresh ways of doing things.

10 Saturday

Waxing

11 Sunday

Waxing

FEBRUARY

M	T	W	T	F	S	S
			1	2	3	4
5	**6**	**7**	**8**	**9**	**10**	**11**
12	13	14	15	16	17	18
19	20	21	22	23	24	25
26	27	28	29			

12 Monday

Waxing

13 Tuesday

Waxing

14 Wednesday

Waxing

Happy Lupercalia (Valentine's Day)! The ancient Roman festival of Lupercalia celebrated virility, wildness, fertility and lust. Today, ride the energetic wave of love of what is now called Valentine's Day and cast a love spell to improve your current relationship or attract a new one that suits you perfectly. Perhaps you will even fall in love with yourself again.

15 Thursday

Waxing

16 Friday

Waxing

17 Saturday

Waxing

18 Sunday

Waxing

FEBRUARY

M	T	W	T	F	S	S
			1	2	3	4
5	6	7	8	9	10	11
12	**13**	**14**	**15**	**16**	**17**	**18**
19	20	21	22	23	24	25
26	27	28	29			

19 Monday

Waxing

20 Tuesday

Waxing

21 Wednesday

Waxing

22 Thursday

Waxing

23 Friday ◑

Waxing

24 Saturday ○ Full moon in Virgo 7.30 am EST

Micro full moon

This is a fantastic time for spells for mental and physical health.

25 Sunday ◐

Waning

Today I woke up grateful.
- sunshine   - Emily
- Pellowship   - Baby Ben

M	T	W	T	F	S	S
			1	2	3	4
5	6	7	8	9	10	11
12	13	14	15	16	17	18
19	**20**	**21**	**22**	**23**	**24**	**25**
26	27	28	29			

26 Monday 🌗

Waning

27 Tuesday 🌗

Waning

28 Wednesday 🌗

Waning

29 Thursday 🌗

Waning

It's a leap year!

1 Friday

Waning

Harvest vegetables that grow below the soil at this time.

2 Saturday

Waning

3 Sunday

Waning

Binding spells are at their most powerful in the waning cycle. What negative behavior would you like to bind?

The light returns;
The icy heart thaws.

– THE GODDESS

FEBRUARY						
M	T	W	T	F	S	S
			1	2	3	4
5	6	7	8	9	10	11
12	13	14	15	16	17	18
19	20	21	22	23	24	25
26	**27**	**28**	**29**			

MARCH						
M	T	W	T	F	S	S
				1	**2**	**3**
4	5	6	7	8	9	10
11	12	13	14	15	16	17
18	19	20	21	22	23	24
25	26	27	28	29	30	31

MARCH

- What would I like to create, experience and manifest this month?

_____

_____

_____

_____

- What are the important dates for me this month?

_____

_____

- What would give me joy this month?

_____

_____

- What am I devoted to?

_____

_____

- Ideas, musings and actions:

_____

_____

_____

SPRING

OPEN AND TRANSFORM

There are few people who don't welcome the relief of spring. We might love winter for all kinds of reasons, but especially after a harsh winter that first feeling of warmth and more light is cheering.

It is in the shoulder seasons – the transformational and transitional seasons of spring and fall – that we humans really experience change. We feel that new start, and we feel the release of the extreme season. Although often easy, sometimes change is hard. The key with a transitional season is to not resist but to flow forward and enjoy the change and the fact that the wheel is turning.

Spring means new growth and birth. Look around you and you'll see different birds that probably have young or soon will. The wind may have turned to another direction. You'll smell fresh plants and experience a certain warmth in the mornings.

Our ancestors were happy about spring because the season brought more food and trade and less hardship. Coming out of winter alive and successful was no mean feat, so it became a season to celebrate with a number of wonderful festivals we can certainly still enjoy if we choose to.

Spring is the perfect time to cast spells for fresh starts, fertility and the success of new projects.

Spring seed ritual

Early spring is a fantastic time to begin to plant seeds,
but make sure you first check that the seeds you wish to plant
do well at this time of year. This beautiful spell will welcome
in spring and also bless and energize the seeds you plant.
Do this spell on a waxing cycle or under a new moon.

Gather together: 2 small quartz crystals that have been
left out under a full moon   some seeds, preferably herbs,
veggies or flowers   water in a watering can or hose.

Open a circle if you wish and say out loud:

*'I humbly speak to the energies of spring. I speak to all the
energies of the changing earth: the wind, the weather, the shorter
nights and the longer days. I welcome in spring!'*

Place the crystals in your hand and focus your awareness on
your feet. Connect with the earth and take three breaths, pulling
up the energy from the earth via your feet. Allow it to flow up
your body and into your hands and into the crystals.

Say:

'I charge these crystals with the power of earth. I add this to the power of the moon.'

Place the seeds in your hand, then repeat the process and say:

'May you grow! May you flourish! May your blossom and fruit!'

Give thanks and close your circle, then plant the seeds and bury the
crystals on each side of the area you have planted the seeds.
The crystals will energise and protect your plants.

Water the seeds.

SEQUANA

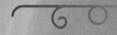

Before the rise of Christianity across Europe each region had its own deities, and some of these were tightly associated with places in nature. Mountains, rivers, springs, caves, forests: all had their spirits and ruling gods or goddesses.

Around the river Seine, way before there was any Paris or major cities, a Gallic tribe called the Sequani worshipped the goddess of that great river, whose name was Sequana. She was most associated with the springs that fed the great river, and it was said that the waters were able to heal the most serious of illnesses.

A healing sanctuary was built to Sequana around 1 BCE, and when the Romans invaded they frequented and honoured the goddess in the sanctuary. In the Roman fashion, tin or wooden objects in the shape of an afflicted body part were offered to the goddess. Pots containing offerings were also recovered from the site, with typical offerings being birds, flowers or coins.

Sequana's associated animal was the duck, and many were found along the areas of the river. Statues of her often depicted the bird, as well as other animals indigenous to the area. She is a cleansing and powerful goddess who can assist in matters of health and vitality.

Spell for flowful health

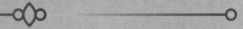

Ahead of time, think about how you want to feel in your body and mind. Additionally, consider what obstacles are in the way of you feeling your very best. For example, you may feel you wish to have more energy, be disease or pain free or simply fitter. Really think about what is in the way, as this will be dealt with in the spell. This spell is best cast during a full or waxing moon phase.

Gather together: a green candle • a large bowl of water • herbs such as a small amount of pine and frankincense resins on charcoal or incense • a pen and paper.

Open a circle or simply relax and center yourself.

Light the candle and say out loud:

'Sequana, you who are flowful and bring bountiful healing to all, I wish for greater health and vitality. I want my body to be completely balanced and I want my body to operate with ease and joy.'

Think about all the obstacles in the way to having a balanced and happy body and mind, and also about how these obstacles prevent you from living as you would most like to. You will probably feel a little negative and pain, regret, sadness or disappointment may arise, but this is natural.

Place your hands in the bowl of water and take a deep breath in. On the exhalation, imagine moving the negative feelings from your body, down your arms, into your hands and into the water.

Say out loud:

'I wash away all obstacles to my health and vitality [wash your hands]. *I wash away these obstacles* [state the obstacles] *now, knowing that you will take them away from me.'*

Leave your hands in the water as long as is necessary to wash away the obstacles.

When that has been done, say:

'I open myself utterly to complete health and abundant vitality. I know I have begun to change for the better and will continue to do so!'

When you are ready, burn the incense or herbs on the charcoal. The fragrant smoke will rise as a gift to Sequana. Use the pen and paper to write down any messages or goals. Blow out the candle.

WHEEL OF THE YEAR

Ostara

Spring equinox 19 March 11.06 pm EST

Ostara is the first equinox of the year, an equinox being when the hours of light and dark are equal. This sacred balance happens twice a year, and ancient peoples celebrated the coming of more light and warmth as a matter of survival. From the day after the spring equinox the sunlight gradually gets stronger and the days longer, creating growth and plenty.

By the time Ostara rolled around it was certainly a busy time on the land, with seeds being well sown and farm animals getting pregnant. The gathering of wild plants to be used as medicine began. If you lived in a place with snow and ice it was now receding and there would be fewer destructive storms. Repairs to homes, buildings and fences and the drying out of dead wood for cooking and heating began and the larger community gathered together and entered into trade.

Ostara is associated with the Germanic goddess Éostre. Her mythos is a very beautiful one that involves her walking through the countryside on a spring morning and bringing warmth back to the land. She found a tiny bird, almost dead from the cold, and she picked it up and tried to warm it. Alas, it is too far gone, so the goddess transformed it into an egg. The egg hatched and a baby bunny was revealed: a symbol of fertility and love. Now you know where the Easter bunny hailed from.

HOW TO CELEBRATE OSTARA

As Ostara is an equinox we usually have the central idea of balance in our minds, but also the idea of progression – remembering that in the next day and the days after until the next equinox there is a shifting towards the light. This reminds us that it is necessary to find moderation and a proper balance for mind, body and spirit. We can look at transforming any habits that are leaning towards the extreme. If we do too much too often and are exhausted, this is the festival that asks us to re-examine how we might more fully balance our time and energy.

Each year I decorate an egg by writing upon it words and images that represent new intentions and fertile wishes for me and my garden, a reminder that 'fertile' can mean prosperity or growth orientation. I go somewhere at the time of the equinox and crack the egg and bury it into the earth. I express gratitude for all that is as I'm casting and for all the expansion that I know now will be. I add some seeds to this area and water it, then when the seeds sprout I give thanks to the goddess again for her signal to me all is moving forward as it should.

4 Monday ☽

Waning

5 Tuesday ☽

Waning

6 Wednesday ☽

Waning

7 Thursday ☽

Waning

8 Friday

Waning

9 Saturday

Dark moon

What would you not like to take into the next lunar cycle? Set it free tonight.

10 Sunday ☽ New moon in Pisces 5.00 am EST

Super new moon

This is a time to cast for greater self-love, acceptance and forgiveness. Use this big new beginnings energy!

You are the magic.

- THE GODDESS

MARCH

M	T	W	T	F	S	S
				1	2	3
4	**5**	**6**	**7**	**8**	**9**	**10**
11	12	13	14	15	16	17
18	19	20	21	22	23	24
25	26	27	28	29	30	31

11 Monday

Waxing

12 Tuesday

Waxing

13 Wednesday

Waxing

14 Thursday

Waxing

Thursday (Thors-day) was named after the Norse god Thor.

15 Friday

Waxing

16 Saturday

Waxing

17 Sunday

Waxing

MARCH
M T W T F S S

				1	2	3
4	5	6	7	8	9	10
11	**12**	**13**	**14**	**15**	**16**	**17**
18	19	20	21	22	23	24
25	26	27	28	29	30	31

18 Monday

Waxing

19 Tuesday Ostara, spring equinox, 11.06 pm EDT

Waxing

This is a time to seek and celebrate balance and to rejoice in this new time of growth and expansion.

20 Wednesday

Waxing

Harvest herbs, fruits and vegetables that grow above the soil at this time.

21 Thursday

Waxing

22 Friday

Waxing

23 Saturday

Waxing

24 Sunday

Waxing

MARCH
M	T	W	T	F	S	S
				1	2	3
4	5	6	7	8	9	10
11	12	13	14	15	16	17
18	**19**	**20**	**21**	**22**	**23**	**24**
25	26	27	28	29	30	31

25 Monday ○ Full moon in Libra 3.00 am EDT

Micro full moon and penumbral lunar eclipse visible in New York

This is a powerful night for spells of balance and ease. Ask for assistance with legal matters if you need it.

26 Tuesday

Waning

27 Wednesday

Waning

28 Thursday

Waning

29 Friday

Waning

30 Saturday

Waning

31 Sunday

Waning

Be secure in your birthright of
being a child of the earth.

- THE GODDESS

MARCH

M	T	W	T	F	S	S
				1	2	3
4	5	6	7	8	9	10
11	12	13	14	15	16	17
18	19	20	21	22	23	24
25	**26**	**27**	**28**	**29**	**30**	**31**

APRIL

◆ What would I like to create, experience and manifest this month?

_____

_____

_____

_____

◆ What are the important dates for me this month?

_____

_____

◆ What would give me joy this month?

_____

_____

◆ What am I devoted to?

_____

_____

◆ Ideas, musings and actions:

_____

_____

_____

BELENUS

GOD OF THE MONTH: APRIL

In almost every mythological framework that features a pantheon of deities there is always at least one whose specialty is healing. Sometimes this is healing of only the physical but often it encompassed all healing, including that of the spirit and the mind. These deities are either associated strongly with the elements of water and fire (light) or they are actual deities of the sun.

Apollo, the Greek god of light, is associated with the sun and is the god who heals and brings wholeness to people but who can paradoxically send plague and disease. The Egyptian god Ra was similar. The goddess Brigid with her healing flame and her holy springs is also a good example of a healing god.

For the ancient Gallic–Celtic peoples the god Belenus (Belenos in Gallic) was a light bringer for those requiring healing. His influence arched from the Italian Peninsula to Britain, with his chief sanctuary being located at the prominent ancient Latin city of Aquilea on the Adriatic coast. He was said to fly across the sky in a chariot, bringing light to the sky. The soldiers of Maximinus Thrax, who laid siege to Aquilea in 238 CE, reported seeing an appearance of the god defending the city from the air.

In ancient times most medicine was herbal, and through archeological finds it is known that Belenus was associated with the healing herb henbane. Henbane is hallucinogenic and was used in rituals for far sight; it may also have been used as an analgesic, sedative and narcotic in some cultures. Healers at sanctuaries doing the work of Belenus needed to be skilled in the use of plants such as henbane as the wrong dosage could result in death.

Belenus was also the god of the eyes and sight, so many people seeking assistance from him had eye afflictions. It was also said that he could cure horses if they were ill. His symbols were horses and chariot wheels and his statues often featured a man with sunrays extending from his head.

SPELL FOR HEALING

AHEAD OF TIME, CONSIDER WHAT AND WHERE YOU REQUIRE HEALING AND WRITE THIS DOWN ON A SLIP OF PAPER. CARRY OUT THIS SPELL OUTSIDE IF POSSIBLE, IN THE DAY TIME; MIDDAY IS BEST.

Gather together: a tealight candle • herbs of any kind; a flame-proof bowl or small cauldron filled with water (aqua solar is great for this).

Light the candle and offer the herbs as a gift.

WITH YOUR ARMS RAISED TO THE SUN, SAY:

'Belenus, bringer of healing and light, I ask you to favor me with your healing power. Illuminate my wounds and make me whole.'

Speak out loud to Belenus what you have written on the paper and offer it to him.

SAY:

'I ask for healing.'

Catch the paper on fire with the flame of the candle, place it in the flame-proof bowl and let it safely burn to ash.

SAY:

'I release this to you.'

Thank Belenus, knowing your words go to him.

Blow out the candle and bury the ashes in the garden.

Take one step towards your own healing no matter how small.

✦

Beltane (Bel Tan, Beltaine)

30 APRIL – 1 MAY

This is the favorite festival of many pagans, for it is a beautiful night full of love and fertility. To ancient peoples the idea of fertility wasn't just about whether or not they could conceive a child: they saw the concept of fertility as something much wider and deeper that extended into nature itself. Fertility was what could be grown, produced and created and represented prosperity in general. In the way that the wheel of the year is balanced, Beltane is the other side of the coin to Samhain (Hallowe'en). While Samhain celebrates death and the power of the void and rest, Beltane embodies life, fullness and fertility in its open aspect.

Bel tan means 'good fire'. Huge torches were lit across Britain and Gaul, and it was said that the fires could be seen miles out to sea. It was a sacred time full of rituals when lushness was brought back to crops, there was adequate rain and life-giving medicinal herbs were plentiful. People travelled to large celebrations and communities got together to celebrate weddings and betrothals. May Day is still celebrated in many modern cultures, normally via picnics and dancing around a maypole. It all looks very innocent, although the origins of these dances were certainly fertility based.

For those who cast it's a great time for spells of fertility of all kinds, health, sexual healing and the conception of ideas and creativity.

HOW TO CELEBRATE BELTANE

The veil between the worlds is now at its thinnest, just as it is at Samhain, so it is one of the two best nights of the year to perform divination. Our ancient and not so ancient ancestors would scry by fire, toss runes or do ogham readings at this time, so pull out your favorite tools of divination and go for it.

Beltane is amazing for powerful potion making, so it is on this day I blend and make all kinds of healing salves, salts and potions. I also like to make magical talismans for healing, the attraction of love and prosperity for my clients. My altar is decorated with flowers and herbs and is very fragrant. As this is a fire festival I place lots of candles in silver, gold and orange colors. I get up very early on Beltane morning and light a candle to celebrate the fiery aspect of this festival. I ask the goddess and god for the energetic blessing of this season and ask that happiness, fertility and love rest upon my house and all in it. I then take my boline into the garden and harvest any of the herbs and flowers I may need for the day's potion making.

If you really want to go with the original style of Beltane you could paint your body with some gold body makeup and fertility symbols and go for a run or dance by the moonlight in your own garden. I know from your feedback that some readers have had a great time doing this, so off you go. Enjoy!

1 Monday

Waning

2 Tuesday

Waning

3 Wednesday

Waning

4 Thursday

Waning

5 Friday ◑

Waning

6 Saturday ◑

Waning

7 Sunday ●

Dark moon

A night of blissful self-care and introspection.

APRIL

M	T	W	T	F	S	S
1	**2**	**3**	**4**	**5**	**6**	**7**
8	9	10	11	12	13	14
15	16	17	18	19	20	21
22	23	24	25	26	27	28
29	30					

8 Monday New moon in Aries 2.20 pm EDT

Super new moon

This powerful new moon will dissipate conflicts and confusion as it is a moon of clarity.

9 Tuesday

Waxing

10 Wednesday

Waxing

11 Thursday

Waxing

12 Friday

Waxing

13 Saturday

Waxing

14 Sunday

Waxing

APRIL

M	T	W	T	F	S	S
1	2	3	4	5	6	7
8	**9**	**10**	**11**	**12**	**13**	**14**
15	16	17	18	19	20	21
22	23	24	25	26	27	28
29	30					

15 Monday

Waxing

16 Tuesday

Waxing

17 Wednesday

Waxing

18 Thursday

Waxing

19 Friday ◑

Waxing

20 Saturday ◑

Waxing

21 Sunday ◑

Waxing

APRIL
M T W T F S S

1	2	3	4	5	6	7
8	9	10	11	12	13	14
15	**16**	**17**	**18**	**19**	**20**	**21**
22	23	24	25	26	27	28
29	30					

22 Monday

Waxing

23 Tuesday ◯ Full moon in Libra 7.48 pm EDT

This is a night to confirm sovereignty and agency over your own life. Set boundaries if you need to.

24 Wednesday

Waning

World Day for Laboratory Animals. Be conscious about products that have animal testing as part of their manufacture – you can choose cruelty free.

25 Thursday

Waning

26 Friday ◐

Waning

27 Saturday ◐

Waning

28 Sunday ◐

Waning

APRIL

M	T	W	T	F	S	S
1	2	3	4	5	6	7
8	9	10	11	12	13	14
15	16	17	18	19	20	21
22	**23**	**24**	**25**	**26**	**27**	**28**
29	30					

 MAY

◆ What would I like to create, experience and manifest this month?

_____

_____

_____

_____

◆ What are the important dates for me this month?

_____

_____

◆ What would give me joy this month?

_____

_____

◆ What am I devoted to?

_____

_____

◆ Ideas, musings and actions:

_____

_____

_____

ISIS

GODDESS OF THE MONTH: MAY

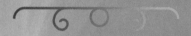

While Isis is one of the most enduring symbols of loving motherhood, dedicated wifehood and feminine protective energy she is also one of the greatest spellcasters of the ancient world. Isis was the daughter of the sky goddess Nut and the earth god Geb, and the cult of Isis spread all over Egypt and extended into Greece and Italy. Major temples were constructed in her honor in Philae and as far as Delos in Greece. Priestesses of Isis were known for their healing and magical skills.

The most famous story of Isis is the story about her healing her husband Osiris. The storm god Set became jealous of his brother Osiris and killed him, in his rage dismembering the body and hiding the pieces so Osiris would not be able to be resurrected. Isis discovered that her husband had been murdered, and her grief was so immense it triggered the flooding of the Nile. Not satisfied that her great love wouldn't attain eternal life, she travelled the earth looking for the pieces of Osiris.

Advised by Thoth, the god of knowledge, Isis cast a powerful spell that brought her husband back to life long enough to conceive a son, Horus. Osiris retreated back into the underworld and Isis became a protectress of the dead, with mighty outstretched wings extending her energy and protecting her body.

When you are fearful or in need of protection call upon this great goddess and allow her wings to surround and protect you. Isis's protective element allows those who work with invocations and magic to do so in confidence, and many practitioners call on her to bless and protect their magical tools.

SPELL TO PROTECT AND DEDICATE MAGICAL TOOLS

SHOULD YOU WISH TO CLEANSE AND DEDICATE A PARTICULAR
ITEM SUCH AS A CARD SET, CRYSTALS AND MAGICAL TOOLS SUCH
AS ATHAMES, HERE IS AN EFFECTIVE SPELL TO DO SO.

Gather together: a gold candle • 1 to 2 milliliters of moon or sun water
in a small bottle • incense • 2 drops of rose or frankincense essential oil in
a teaspoon of carrier oil in a shallow dish.

Ahead of time, decide what or who your tool or item will
be dedicated to and place the item on your altar.

LIGHT THE CANDLE AND SAY:

*'Mighty Isis, you whose wings enfold us, I ask that this tool be dedicated
to* [state your intention]. *I ask that its energies align with mine.'*

POUR THE MAGICAL MOON OR SUN WATER ON YOUR HANDS AND SAY:

'I cleanse any negativity from my presence. I banish all that needs not be there.'

Sprinkle the object with some of the water on your hand; just flick a little
into the air if the object can be damaged by the water in any way.

SAY:

'I cleanse this [whatever it is]. *I banish all that needs not be
there and I create a fresh clean space to dedicate into.'*

Light the incense and allow the smoke to pass over the item.
Hold the item in your hand and think only of your positive
intention. Breathe deeply and relax into this, then pass the item
though the fragrant smoke coming from the resins and herbs.

SAY:

'I dedicate this to [state your intention] *and I know this power
weaves with mine for the greatest good of all. This now becomes
a tool of power in full use of my magic. So mote it be!'*

Rub the essential oil blend over your hands and allow some
of it to touch the item but not damage it in any way.

Thank Isis for her blessing and protection
and blow out the candle.

29 Monday

Waning

30 Tuesday

Waning

1 Wednesday

Waning

Happy Beltane! Celebrate the good (bel) fire (tan) and delight in the most fertile of spring energies and growth today and tonight. Decorate your altar with fresh flowers or make a maypole in your yard.

2 Thursday

Waning

3 Friday

Waning

4 Saturday

Waning

Plant seeds for above-ground growers such as lettuce, cabbage and mint.

5 Sunday

Waning

| APRIL | | | | | | | MAY | | | | | | |
M	T	W	T	F	S	S	M	T	W	T	F	S	S
1	2	3	4	5	6	7			1	2	3	4	5
8	9	10	11	12	13	14	6	7	8	9	10	11	12
15	16	17	18	19	20	21	13	14	15	16	17	18	19
22	23	24	25	26	27	28	20	21	22	23	24	25	26
29	**30**						27	28	29	30	31		

6 Monday

Dark moon

Release your fears and burdens.

7 Tuesday New moon in Taurus 11.21 pm EDT

Find pleasure again! Determine what makes you really happy and set intentions to do more of this.

8 Wednesday

Waxing

9 Thursday

Waxing

10 Friday ◑

Waxing

11 Saturday ◑

Waxing

12 Sunday ◑

Waxing

MAY
M	T	W	T	F	S	S
		1	2	3	4	5
6	**7**	**8**	**9**	**10**	**11**	**12**
13	14	15	16	17	18	19
20	21	22	23	24	25	26
27	28	29	30	31		

13 Monday ◑

Waxing

14 Tuesday ◑

Waxing

Tuesday was named after Twia, the Celtic/Germanic god of war and the sky. The Norse god Týr is also closely identified with this day.

15 Wednesday ◑

Waxing

16 Thursday ◑

Waxing

17 Friday ◐

Waxing

18 Saturday ◐

Waxing

19 Sunday ◐

Waxing

MAY

M	T	W	T	F	S	S
		1	2	3	4	5
6	7	8	9	10	11	12
13	**14**	**15**	**16**	**17**	**18**	**19**
20	21	22	23	24	25	26
27	28	29	30	31		

20 Monday ◐

Waxing

21 Tuesday ◐

Waxing

22 Wednesday ◐

Waxing

23 Thursday ○ Full moon in Scorpio 9.53 am EDT

This is a powerful night to cast spells for self-empowerment and better relationships.

24 Friday ☽

Waning

25 Saturday ☽

Waning

26 Sunday ☽

Waning

MAY

M	T	W	T	F	S	S
		1	2	3	4	5
6	7	8	9	10	11	12
13	14	15	16	17	18	19
20	**21**	**22**	**23**	**24**	**25**	**26**
27	28	29	30	31		

27 Monday ☽

Waning

28 Tuesday ☽

Waning

29 Wednesday ☽

Waning

30 Thursday ☽

Waning

31 Friday

Waning

1 Saturday

Waning

2 Sunday

Waning

MAY							JUNE						
M	**T**	**W**	**T**	**F**	**S**	**S**	**M**	**T**	**W**	**T**	**F**	**S**	**S**
		1	2	3	4	5						1	2
6	7	8	9	10	11	12	3	4	5	6	7	8	9
13	14	15	16	17	18	19	10	11	12	13	14	15	16
20	21	22	23	24	25	26	17	18	19	20	21	22	23
27	**28**	**29**	**30**	**31**			24	25	26	27	28	29	30

JUNE

- ◆ What would I like to create, experience and manifest this month?

_____

_____

_____

_____

- ◆ What are the important dates for me this month?

_____

_____

- ◆ What would give me joy this month?

_____

_____

- ◆ What am I devoted to?

_____

_____

- ◆ Ideas, musings and actions:

_____

_____

_____

SUMMER

The pulsating peak

This is the most expansive time of the year, and we can feel summer's aliveness and extroversion coming. If the weather isn't too extreme we can make plans to go outside and take advantage of the warmer season; in fact, more people are usually out and about at this time. We also linger outside at night time, and where I live on a full moon night the beaches are crowded with people enjoying the balmy evening and having lunar picnics.

My garden is absolutely alive both day and night. There is so much sound, with birds calling and cicadas singing their radical vibrating songs. The plants are growing before your eyes and there are so many insects of all kinds. The days are languid and long and it's hard to remember the rigidity of winter.

It's tempting to think as a beginner does that the cold, scary, dark times of winter are the best for magic, but that is just a stereotype. I know that each season has its joys and focuses but that summer, due to its huge stored energy, is incredibly powerful for magical practice. Real magic is an alchemic activity that weaves different elements together (including the element of 'us') towards an intention, so the bigger the energy the easier it might be to capture and direct.

Big energy; big magic.

I recommend that you cast for health and vitality, relationships of all kinds, career success and prosperity. I also ensure I take the time at a dark moon phase in summer to ensure I let go of what I don't need. I want a clear run at my intentions, and that's hard if I'm carrying burdens or unnecessary fears. I love the happier, lighter vibe of summer and I'll cast for happiness and more pleasure. I'll also go skyclad more often in my workings, and the sensual nature of the season encourages outdoor casting and casting by the sea.

GET YOUR SPARKLE ON:
MIDSUMMER MAGIC

CALL ME A KID IF YOU LIKE, BUT I LOVE THE BIG MAGIC OF
MIDSUMMER'S EVE. I ENJOY THE WHOLE CONCEPT OF IT, THE HISTORY
AND THE RITUALS, AND I KNOW MANY OF YOU DO AS WELL.

I've mentioned previously how my grandmother enlightened me about midsummer
and the way ancient peoples traveled to the solstice festival while watching out for
the good people, the fae. She explained that they would be on the paths and roads on
the way to a big regional community festival and it might take a day or night to get
there. They would take food and perhaps things to trade and camp out. There would
be feasting and probably a fair bit of storytelling and drinking, but they had to keep
their wits about them because midsummer's eve was a big night for the fae. If anyone
did the wrong thing and disrespected the fae or their places they might be swept away
and never heard from again.

The ancients had a healthy respect for the fae, who to them weren't just pretty
and sweet faery figures. They could play a trick on you, take something valuable to
you or even kill you, so travellers, especially on this night, were mindful of their
behavior and made offerings to the fae along the way.

I love my garden, so on midsummer's eve I give thanks to the wee fae who help
take care of it. Since I was a small child I have prepared little gifts for this night.
I normally have small plates of food for them that feature fat strawberries, honey,
cream, sweets or cakes. I also place sparkly objects, flowers, glittery ribbons and
crystals in places I think they may frequent.

I loved doing this when I was small and all kids love to leave gifts out for the fae, so
involve them. Children often have an instinctive feel for where the fae might frequent,
so let them be the location finders for where to leave your presents. As I leave the
plates I thank the fae, and magically mostly bare plates are left in the morning.

NIKE

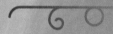

One of the most famous statues to grace the halls of the Louvre in Paris is that of the goddess Nike, the Winged Victory of Samothrace. It is one of the most inspiring of ancient sculptures, and even though it is incomplete you can still get a feeling of the power, momentum and inspiration Nike brings towards victory – in this case a military one.

Nike was both an independent entity in her own right and later an aspect of Athena particularly and sometimes Zeus. She features in some of the earliest of Greek mythology and especially in the story of the battle between the Olympian gods and the Titans.

One Titan, Typhon, was a terrible monster who during the battle made his way to Olympus to make his final attack. All the other gods had fled from the mountain and Zeus was alone, sitting frightened and unsure what to do next. Nike flew to his aid to tell him that he must have courage and be a champion for his kind. She also reminded him that should Typhon win he would rape both of Zeus's daughters, Athena and Artemis. Nike told Zeus to gather his weapons of storms and thunderbolts and do everything he could to achieve victory. Her words inspired Zeus and he fought a ferocious battle against Typhon, eventually subduing him and becoming master of the universe as it was.

Nike was involved in most aspects of any activity where a win or victory was important, such as in the military and sports. At Olympia, the home of the Olympic Games, next to Zeus's altar was an altar dedicated solely to Nike. If you visit the Acropolis in Athens today you can visit the temple of Athena/Nike. Nike was an important goddess for the Athenians and one they made sure to devote themselves to because of the martial history of the city.

RITUAL FOR VICTORY

WHENEVER YOU DO WORKINGS FOR VICTORY OR WINNING ANYTHING IT IS IMPORTANT YOU ARE ETHICAL: YOU SHOULD NEVER CAST FOR SOMEONE'S DESTRUCTION OR HURT. THIS IS FOR YOUR VICTORY AND SUCCESS IF IT BE FOR THE GOOD OF ALL. THE BEST TIME TO CAST IS EITHER DURING A WAXING OR FULL MOON PHASE AND OUTDOORS IN THE TRADITIONAL GREEK STYLE.

Gather together: a gold candle • incense • a glass of wine • a handful of grain such as millet, wheat or, at a pinch, rice.

Light the candle and burn the incense.

Center yourself, taking three deep breaths, and think of Nike's inspiration and power.

Take another three breaths and think about your situation and where you want victory. Think only about yourself, not your competition or obstacle. Think about your victory and how it will feel, what you have done to get where you are and how you deserve a victory.

POUR A LITTLE OF THE WINE ON THE EARTH AND SAY:

'I offer my libation first to Queen Hera.'
[Many traditional Hellenic workings offer to Hera first.]

TOSS THE GRAIN ON THE GROUND AND SAY:

'Great goddess Nike, I offer the fruits of the land to you.'

POUR THE REST OF THE WINE ON THE EARTH AND SAY:

'Great goddess of victory, please accept this libation. Grant me my victory [tell Nike of your situation]. *I ask humbly that I am victorious!'*

Close your eyes and again visualize your victory and the goddess coming to your aid and inspiration. Thank her and blow out the candle.

WHEEL OF THE YEAR

Litha, summer solstice

20 June 4.50 pm EDT

Litha is a solstice festival in which the longest day of the year and the shortest night are experienced. It is power-full. The importance of this day is even built into the architectural alignments of many ancient temples and constructions, including Egyptian and Mayan pyramids and stone circles such as Stonehenge, and it's a key agricultural marker for growth. We know where we are in the year, and in sacred terms we are at full solar peak and magical power.

There is a precious immediacy about Litha; it is a focus on now. Just think: the heat is here, the power is here and everything has been building to this moment, Accordingly, we should take advantage of this and not waste a moment. Litha enables us to be the conduit for our birthright of vitality and peak energy. I can always feel Litha approaching because the energy I regularly pull up from the earth to do workings has a certain strength and tone. It is big and expansive and thrums with life. This strength of flow lends itself to workings for prosperity and for our health.

As Litha is a pulsing sun festival it allows a big solar light to burn away your health imbalances and prompts you to make better choices for your well-being. The big sun-driven energy lends itself to inviting in vitality and good health.

HOW TO CELEBRATE LITHA

Litha is a long, long day, but don't waste a moment of this energy! Get up at dawn, light a candle and give thanks for all you have. I go outside and pull up some of that amazing Litha energy from the earth. I allow the mighty expansion of that energy upwards throughout my body to flow through me for as long as it feels good, then I ensure I make offerings to all the gods I work with in gratitude for their love and support.

One of my favourite things to do is have a sunset picnic with like-minded friends. We prepare great food to share and charge up coins to leave as random gifts for strangers to share our joy and prosperity. This is also the best day of the year to make aqua sol (sun water) because of the long daylight hours. Aqua sol is made by leaving out a bowl of water from midday until sunset then popping it into a water bottle that will keep it fresh, and it's useful in potions and spells for health and vitality and also for protection of the home.

3 Monday ◑

Waning

4 Tuesday ◑

Waning

5 Wednesday ●

Dark moon

Delight in a quiet night in, allowing yourself some solo time that is rich with pleasure.

6 Thursday ☽ New moon in Gemini 8.37 am EDT

Dream big, considering ways to expand your world, travel or express yourself more fully.

7 Friday ◑

Waxing

8 Saturday ◑

Waxing

9 Sunday ◑

Waxing

Flow like water.

- THE GODDESS

JUNE

JUNE

M	T	W	T	F	S	S
					1	2
3	**4**	**5**	**6**	**7**	**8**	**9**
10	11	12	13	14	15	16
17	18	19	20	21	22	23
24	25	26	27	28	29	30

10 Monday

Waxing

11 Tuesday

Waxing

12 Wednesday

Waxing

13 Thursday

Waxing

14 Friday

Waxing

15 Saturday

Waxing

You might like to prepare your wishes and celebrations for Litha, which is coming next week!

16 Sunday

Waxing

I didn't make you to be everyone's
cup of tea.

– THE GODDESS

JUNE

M	T	W	T	F	S	S
					1	2
3	4	5	6	7	8	9
10	**11**	**12**	**13**	**14**	**15**	**16**
17	18	19	20	21	22	23
24	25	26	27	28	29	30

17 Monday

Waxing

18 Tuesday

Waxing

19 Wednesday

Waxing

Get your magic on tonight, for it is midsummer's eve! We honor the fae in our gardens and wild places this evening, so start your preparations early. This is a wonderful festival to involve your kids, because who doesn't love a faery? Traditional gifts of strawberries, honey and milk plus glittery objects are left out in wild places for the local fae. Give thanks to them for the protective work they do in your environment.

20 Thursday Litha, summer solstice, 4.50 pm EDT

Waxing

It's the summer solstice, the longest day of the year and the shortest night. It is a time of peak energy and an ideal day to do workings for health, vitality and prosperity.

21 Friday ◯ Full moon in Capricorn 9.07 pm EDT

Being so close to the solstice, take advantage of the energy to set big goals for more prosperity in your work life.

22 Saturday ◑

Waning

23 Sunday ◑

Waning

Be your own alchemist.

- THE GODDESS

JUNE

M	T	W	T	F	S	S
					1	2
3	4	5	6	7	8	9
10	11	12	13	14	15	16
17	**18**	**19**	**20**	**21**	**22**	**23**
24	25	26	27	28	29	30

24 Monday

Waning

25 Tuesday

Waning

26 Wednesday

Waning

This is a good day to trim your hair if you want to keep the same style for longer.

27 Thursday

Waning

28 Friday 🌓

Waning

29 Saturday 🌓

Waning

30 Sunday 🌓

Waning

Feel the pulse of the universe
For it is also yours.

– THE GODDESS

JUNE

M	T	W	T	F	S	S
					1	2
3	4	5	6	7	8	9
10	11	12	13	14	15	16
17	18	19	20	21	22	23
24	**25**	**26**	**27**	**28**	**29**	**30**

JULY

◆ What would I like to create, experience and manifest this month?

_____

_____

_____

_____

◆ What are the important dates for me this month?

_____

_____

◆ What would give me joy this month?

_____

_____

◆ What am I devoted to?

_____

_____

◆ Ideas, musings and actions:

_____

_____

_____

MANANNÁN MAC LIR

GOD OF THE MONTH: JULY

In the mythos of the Irish, Manannán mac Lir is a part of the old gods called the Tuatha Dé Danann and is a god of the sea. He is known under slightly different names by the Welsh and Scottish, and the Isle of Man is named for him. His name means 'son of the sea' and his wife is the beautiful Frand of the faeries.

Manannán mac Lir is a figure who appears frequently in old mythos and has many roles to play, often that of protector or as a kind of trickster. In folklore of the 17th and 18th centuries it is said that mac Lir will defend Irish honor against the English, and there are countless stories of trickery that result in an underdog Irish win. He had a magical shield, golden apples and enchanted swine and was famous for being able to conjure a cloak of invisibility that he could extend over the land and his people to protect them.

After the Tuatha Dé Danann were defeated by the human Érimón, Manannán was chosen as co-king of the remaining Tuatha Dé Danann. He had the sad task of allotting which *sidhes* (fae mounds) the survivors would be settled into. Manannán made sure that his people were safe by concealing them all in the *féth fiada* (mist of invisibility). He then held a sacred feast of Goibniu, which gave them all eternal youth, and gave them his magical swine, which ensured they would be fed forever.

At some time in our lives we all need some protection and help and the good thinking and wisdom of other people. It has always been this way, and this is what Manannán offers if we ask.

RITUAL FOR PROTECTION

I PREFER TO CAST THIS SPELL ON A DARK OR NEW MOON, BUT ANY
TIME YOU NEED IT IS THE BEST TIME. YOU CAN GO DOWN TO THE
SEA TO CAST SO THAT YOU ARE CLOSE TO MANANNÁN.

Gather together: 3 silver or green candles (tealight candles are fine if you don't have the correct colors) • a glass of wine, honey, mead or cider • a glass of sea water or ordinary water with 1 teaspoon of salt added.

LIGHT ONE CANDLE AND SAY:

*'Manannán mac Lir, I call thee. I ask for your protection.
I ask you to turn your eyes upon me.'*

OFFER THE WINE TO THE GOD, THEN LIGHT THE SECOND CANDLE AND SAY:

*'Son of the sea, great protector, I light the flame in your name.
I ask that like the great mist you willed for the Tuatha you
also protect and shield me* [explain your situation].*'*

LIGHT THE THIRD CANDLE AND SAY:

*'Manannán mac Lir, you who bring calm and peace to difficult situations,
provide wisdom for me and shield me from the chaos of others.'*

POUR THE SALT WATER OVER YOUR HANDS AND SAY:

*'I wash away my anxieties and burden, knowing you will assist
me. I trust all will be well and I will act in your guidance.'*

Allow any guidance or messages to come to you.

When you are ready, blow out each candle and give thanks.

1 Monday ◑

Waning

2 Tuesday ◑

Waning

3 Wednesday ◑

Waning

4 Thursday ●

Dark moon

5 Friday 🌙 New moon in Cancer 6.57 pm EDT

This night will illuminate your shadows and transform them.

6 Saturday

Waxing

Under the dreamy new moon, set intentions for creativity and growth.

7 Sunday

Waxing

We are all part of the great circle.

- THE GODDESS

JULY

M	T	W	T	F	S	S
1	**2**	**3**	**4**	**5**	**6**	**7**
8	9	10	11	12	13	14
15	16	17	18	19	20	21
22	23	24	25	26	27	28
29	30	31				

8 Monday ◐

Waxing

9 Tuesday ◐

Waxing

10 Wednesday ◐

Waxing

11 Thursday ◐

Waxing

12 Friday

Waxing

13 Saturday

Waxing

14 Sunday

Waxing

Just as the sun rises
So will you.

– THE GODDESS

M	T	W	T	F	S	S
1	2	3	4	5	6	7
8	**9**	**10**	**11**	**12**	**13**	**14**
15	16	17	18	19	20	21
22	23	24	25	26	27	28
29	30	31				

15 Monday

Waxing

Harvest above-ground vegetables this week.

16 Tuesday

Waxing

17 Wednesday

Waxing

18 Thursday

Waxing

19 Friday

Waxing

20 Saturday

Waxing

21 Sunday ◯ Full moon in Capricorn 6.17 am EDT

This is a night to plan big things and put structures in place to achieve this. Cast BIG magic.

Ground yourself, place your feet
Upon the earth and breathe.

– THE GODDESS

JULY

M	T	W	T	F	S	S
1	2	3	4	5	6	7
8	9	10	11	12	13	14
15	**16**	**17**	**18**	**19**	**20**	**21**
22	23	24	25	26	27	28
29	30	31				

22 Monday ◐

Waning

23 Tuesday ◐

Waning

24 Wednesday ◐

Waning

25 Thursday ◐

Waning

Harvest under-ground vegetables this week.

26 Friday 🌔

Waning

27 Saturday 🌔

Waning

28 Sunday 🌔

Waning

Deep and flowing
Unlimited
My love for you.

- THE GODDESS

JULY

M	T	W	T	F	S	S
1	2	3	4	5	6	7
8	9	10	11	12	13	14
15	16	17	18	19	20	21
22	**23**	**24**	**25**	**26**	**27**	**28**
29	30	31				

AUGUST

◆ What would I like to create, experience and manifest this month?

_____

_____

_____

_____

◆ What are the important dates for me this month?

_____

_____

_____

◆ What would give me joy this month?

_____

_____

_____

◆ What am I devoted to?

_____

_____

_____

◆ Ideas, musings and actions:

_____

_____

_____

VÍÐARR

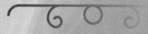

Viðarr, one of the 12 Norse high gods, is an Æsir and a son of Odin and the jötunn Griðr. He is described as having a thick iron shoe and great strength and sits upon his throne usually in wisdom and silence. He rides a horse and has a beautiful kingdom of high grasses. He is associated with vengeance and silence, both of which are described in his mythos.

Viðarr features in one of Norse mythology's most complex and, I think, beautiful stories. His father Odin, the ruler of the 12 high gods, has insight into Ragnarök, or the end of the world. He understands some of what will happen but not all, and he foretells that he will very probably die but that his son will avenge him. In Norse society vengeance is part of the law but it has to happen in a balanced way, otherwise it is an offence to the gods. It is not strictly an eye for an eye – in fact, there are records of deaths being avenged by the taking of land rather than lives – but it certainly is part of the code of the times.

When Ragnarök happened the all father Odin was killed by the great wolf Fenrir. Víðarr, often referred to as the 'silent one', held a vow of silence before fighting to the death with Fenrir. It is theorized that as a part of ritual mourning and the consideration of justice the avenger holds a ritual silence for a time. Víðarr took his iron-clad shoe and placed it on the bottom jaw and forked tongue of the massive beast, then used his spear and strength to stab the monster wolf and rip his mouth apart.

We must be careful to seek clear justice, not revenge. Víðarr survived Ragnarök and heralded in a cycle of rebirth.

A MEDITATION ON SILENCE

MANY CULTURES AND SPIRITUAL PATHWAYS HAVE SILENCE AS A RECOMMENDED
KEY ACTION FOR WELL-BEING. IN OUR BUSY WORLD, BEING ABLE TO
KEEP AND HOLD THE SPACE OF SILENCE FOR OURSELVES IS A RARE THING
AS THERE IS SO MUCH NOISE AND DISTRACTION AROUND US.

To be able to make wise choices and for decision-making we need a space between stimulus and reaction. This can be as little as a heartbeat or as long as many days, but if we don't create that space and particularly in difficult or triggering situations we go straight into reaction, which is not always the best action.

Víðarr enacted a period of ritual silence before acting. He observed, he took counsel, he planned and he prepared. Here is a meditation featuring Víðarr, and it is something I like to do around the time of a dark moon.

Close your eyes, get yourself into a comfortable position and breathe deeply. Relax and put any worries or your to-do list, which you can come back to later if you wish. Just concentrate on your breathing.

Imagine the Norseman Víðarr on his throne: he is calm and peaceful but alert and powerful. He has gravitas and authority but he says nothing. All is silent. You too are silent. Consider where silence would have been a wise action. We don't always have to speak or give an opinion: we can give ourselves sacred space between stimulus and reaction.

Allow your mind to search for a time when giving yourself space and silence would have helped you. There is no judgement, just observation. Allow yourself to feel into the silence, which may feel disconcerting, unusual or even irritating but make sure you let it happen because it might also feel peaceful and free.

See Víðarr once more, feeling into the power of his silence and the wisdom that comes with it. He nods to you in recognition and blessing.

When you are ready, come back to where you are, into your own self and in the now. Stay as silent as you can and be gentle with yourself.

THE WHEEL OF THE YEAR

✦

Lammas

Lammas is the first of the harvest festivals for the year. Harvest times were often very community driven. Whole villages and communities came together to assist each other gather the food and feast upon it. Groups hunted together and shared what they killed, and medicinal herbs were gathered by healers and teaching to the young people about this medicine was done. It was about the collective good, not just the singular good.

I love the harvest festivals because they give me an excuse to feel grateful in a practical way and to examine more deeply how I'm progressing in life. To look back and see how far we've come in the last month, year, couple of years – even decades – is something we should all feel good about doing, because in this way we can see what is working for us and what is not and change things if we have a negative pattern going on. Marking our successes gives us confidence and an evidence base that we do indeed achieve what we want, things do go right for us and the world turns for us! This is incredibly worthwhile.

It's time to cook and eat all the fresh food that has been harvested, so invite your friends around to eat and swap stories about their own personal harvests.

HOW TO CELEBRATE LAMMAS

My Lammas altar reflects the harvest of that time of year. We all live in different locations and I think it's modern and beneficial to feature foods that are seasonal where you are. Traditionally, however, the Lammas altar was one with baked goods and certainly bread. I decorate a pretty basket and add freshly baked bread and maybe a cake or two, as well as nuts and fruits of the season.

I start the day by baking bread; I'm no baker but I try, and it always smells so delicious and makes my house somehow more welcoming. I normally try to prepare the dough and let it rise the night before and then bake it Lammas morning. I know some of you are incredible bakers and I see your work on my social media pages, so keep it going! The gods and goddesses no doubt appreciate your amazing ability.

If I do decide to have a dinner with friends, everyone brings something to add and eat. This way we are doing what some of our ancestors would have done. Our table is decorated in fall colors and we have flowers of the season. Our ritual is normally a simple one: one of gratitude for what we have and for each other. We speak about all we are thankful for and all we have achieved and end with a mighty 'Huzzah!'

29 Monday

Waning

30 Tuesday

Waning

31 Wednesday

Waning

1 Thursday

Waning

Lammas: the first of the harvest festivals is a time to feel real gratitude for the harvest of your own life. Bake bread and get together with friends.

2 Friday

Waning

3 Saturday

Dark moon

This is a night to undertake extreme self-care; perhaps run a relaxing potion-filled bath.

4 Sunday ☽ New moon in Leo 7.13 am EDT

Make a powerful new start around personal relationships. Cast to enrich your relationships or to start afresh.

Delight in your strengths
Transform your shadows.
Both are beautiful.

- THE GODDESS

JULY								AUGUST					
M	**T**	**W**	**T**	**F**	**S**	**S**		**M**	**T**	**W**	**T**	**F**	**S**	**S**
1	2	3	4	5	6	7					**1**	**2**	**3**	**4**
8	9	10	11	12	13	14		5	6	7	8	9	10	11
15	16	17	18	19	20	21		12	13	14	15	16	17	18
22	23	24	25	26	27	28		19	20	21	22	23	24	25
29	**30**	**31**						26	27	28	29	30	31

5 Monday

Waxing

6 Tuesday

Waxing

7 Wednesday

Waxing

8 Thursday

Waxing

9 Friday

Waxing

10 Saturday

Waxing

11 Sunday

Waxing

AUGUST

M	T	W	T	F	S	S
			1	2	3	4
5	**6**	**7**	**8**	**9**	**10**	**11**
12	13	14	15	16	17	18
19	20	21	22	23	24	25
26	27	28	29	30	31	

12 Monday

Waxing

13 Tuesday

Waxing

14 Wednesday

Waxing

15 Thursday

Waxing

16 Friday

Waxing

17 Saturday

Waxing

18 Sunday

Waxing

AUGUST						
M	T	W	T	F	S	S
			1	2	3	4
5	6	7	8	9	10	11
12	**13**	**14**	**15**	**16**	**17**	**18**
19	20	21	22	23	24	25
26	27	28	29	30	31	

19 Monday ◯ Full moon in Aquarius 2.25 pm EDT

This inventive full moon is perfect for setting intentions for creativity, innovation and the greater good.

20 Tuesday ◗

Waning

21 Wednesday ◗

Waning

22 Thursday ◗

Waning

23 Friday

Waning

24 Saturday

Waning

25 Sunday

Waning

AUGUST

M	T	W	T	F	S	S
			1	2	3	4
5	6	7	8	9	10	11
12	13	14	15	16	17	18
19	**20**	**21**	**22**	**23**	**24**	**25**
26	27	28	29	30	31	

26 Monday ☽

Waning

27 Tuesday ☽

Waning

28 Wednesday ☽

Waning

The warmth and light are retreating and it's time to make some changes! Simplify? A seasonal diet change?

29 Thursday ☽

Waning

30 Friday ◐

Waning

31 Saturday ◐

Waning

1 Sunday ●

Dark moon

Let. It. Go.

Open your senses

Observe your connection.

- THE GODDESS

AUGUST							SEPTEMBER						
M	**T**	**W**	**T**	**F**	**S**	**S**	**M**	**T**	**W**	**T**	**F**	**S**	**S**
			1	2	3	4							1
5	6	7	8	9	10	11	2	3	4	5	6	7	8
12	13	14	15	16	17	18	9	10	11	12	13	14	15
19	20	21	22	23	24	25	16	17	18	19	20	21	22
26	**27**	**28**	**29**	**30**	**31**		23	24	25	26	27	28	29
							30						

SEPTEMBER

◆ What would I like to create, experience and manifest this month?

_____

_____

_____

_____

◆ What are the important dates for me this month?

_____

_____

◆ What would give me joy this month?

_____

_____

◆ What am I devoted to?

_____

_____

◆ Ideas, musings and actions:

_____

_____

_____

FALL

Fall is the part of the earth cycle we often can really see visually. We quickly pick up on the change in color of the leaves as they turn orange and brown. We see the sky lose its impossible bright blue. We perceive longer shadows and the daylight hours shorten. We also feel the change of fall. Mornings and evenings cool and the arc of the sun changes, as does wind direction. We start to get a more unsettled pattern to the weather – one day hot, one day cold – and it's not just the weather that gets unsettled: often we do as well.

Change isn't always easy. Here we are enjoying the ease of summer only to have it seemingly snatched away from us just as we are getting used to it. All that delicious expansion and openness is now being pulled back into itself. Our bodies can feel achy and rigid as the fall season approaches because it is hard to adapt fast enough. Fall, then, is really a time to focus on your body and health. Make sure you change your diet to a more seasonal one and that what you eat is nourishing and kind to your body. Ensure you get enough movement: do something creative and flowful.

Fall traditionally was the season not only for harvest but for preparation. Winter isn't that far away, and while we can we should begin to plan for what we want to experience during the next few months going into winter, along with an emphasis on ridding ourselves of outdated paradigms and beliefs.

Fall blessing for change

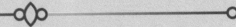

Ahead of time, take a few minutes to think about what you want for the several months before wintertime. Make sure this is a planning format, that it's not just a daydream: commit what you want to paper. On a separate sheet of paper, also write down what you no longer wish to bring forward. Certain reactions, burdens, worries and patterns: now is the time of change to cast to let them go.

Gather together: a candle • incense • a flameproof bowl.

Do this spell outside if possible and during a full or new moon phase. With your written-down plan in hand and your list of things to release, open a circle in the manner you choose.

Light the candle and say:

'Energies of fall, help me transform what is into what I wish.'

Burn the incense and pass the list of what you want through the fragrant smoke.

Read what you want out loud with feeling and say:

'May this be so.'

Read out loud the list of what you wish to release then say:

'May this be transformed into positive change.'

Burn the list and safely drop it into the flame-proof bowl. Allow it to burn to ashes and allow the wind to catch the ashes and take them.

Blow out the candle and give thanks.

UZUME

Uzume is a much-loved Japanese Shinto goddess of laughter and happiness. She is the sister of the mighty Amaterasu, the sun goddess. These sisters are the most beloved of the Japanese deities and there is a rich series of myths surrounding them, but the story I'll share seems like a sad one at first although it has a happy and beautiful ending.

Amaterasu lived a peaceful life very much in harmony with the workings of nature, shining brightly among her herd of horses and gardens full of silkworms for her weaving. However, her brother, Susanowa, was much more disruptive and chaotic. Susanowa became jealous of his sister's power and slaughtered her horses and silkworms, and when Amaterasu came upon such a gruesome and shocking scene she became so full of grief and hopelessness that she retreated into a cave. This left the earth with no sun and everything grew cold and dead. The earthly plane became a haven for evil spirits that terrified everyone, and the people began to die from the lack of food.

The other gods and the people waited outside Amaterasu's cave and tried everything to get her to come out again. She refused, as she wished to never show her face again. As things grew desperate, Uzume had an idea: she asked some of the other gods to play music and she began to dance a bawdy dance, lifting up her skirts and singing comically. She began to tell jokes and laugh loudly, which bought a roar of approval from the assembled crowd.

The loud, joyful commotion and laughter was heard ringing across the world and Amaterasu became curious and decided to peep out of her cave. Uzume was prepared for this and had placed a mirror just outside the cave. When the bright light of dawn that was the Amaterasu's energy hit the mirror the goddess became bedazzled by her own reflection, and her giggling sister was able to pull her out of the cave. The world became a better place again because of her presence, and Amaterasu gleaned her true worth.

Call upon the laughing Uzume when you need a lift and to lighten your mood. If you are feeling low and sad, Uzume will lead the way out of the darkness.

Invocation to Uzume for happiness

Ahead of time, think about a few things that make you happy.

Gather together: an orange or yellow candle • incense • a small hand mirror.

Put on some music that always lifts your mood and play it loud!

Light the candle and incense and say:

'I honor you, Uzume. I ask you to turn your attention upon me. I honor you with this piece of music that I hope pleases you. I come before you today to ask you for your blessings of happiness upon me.'

Begin to dance to the music you love. Let yourself go and be taken by the music. Do this as long as you like and feel the happiness rise.

At the peak of this experience, clap three times and jump into the air.

Clap three times again and allow the feeling of happiness and wonder to spread through every cell of your body. Flood your body with goodwill and gratitude.

When you are ready, open your eyes and say:

'I ask that I remember the happiness and laughter I feel right now. I thank you, Uzume, for the blessing of this moment of fun and beauty and joy.'

Clap three times and say:

'It is as I have asked.'

Look at yourself in the mirror, at your face and the feeling of joy reflecting upon the world!

WHEEL OF THE YEAR

Mabon: fall equinox

22 SEPTEMBER 8.43 AM EDT

The days are growing shorter and we are at the fall equinox, a time of balance and beauty. With an equinox there is a perfect balance between the elements of light and dark, and from this time onwards until Ostara the hours of light will incrementally shorten.

Mabon is the second of the harvest festivals and the final one before winter places its icy hands on the land. We have a chance now to consider what we need to do to prepare for harder times and to make sure we have enough to survive. Homes, fences and halls were repaired and strengthened to withstand the oncoming winter storms and joint activities were held among communities to make sure everyone was prepared.

This was a time when food began to be preserved, fruits gathered and dried and jams made. The smoking house was busy preserving the hunt, and medicinal herbs were gathered and dried ready for the people during the winter when they would most need it. The last hive checks and harvesting of honey also happened, and this was often the last time big groups of regional people met and engaged in trade.

HOW TO CELEBRATE MABON

As this is an equinox it is an especially magical time to cast. I love to cast spells for successful work and for the greater good, and I again look at the concept of balance in my life and how I can improve this.

As the earth cools I harvest the last of my medicinal herbs and leave plenty of foliage for the health of the plant. I dry the herbs and flower petals I do not use in the stronger fall winds and trim back some of my plants so they can rest for winter. Just as the elders did back then I make good use of the fall produce, preparing jams and chutneys. I have to say that opening one of those jars of goodness in the middle of winter is such a sensual treat! As with Lammas this is also a time to bake, although now it's heavier treats such as cakes and biscuits often redolent with honey.

My altar features gold, brown and bronze colors and I use my black and white stones to signify balance. I might place some pretty fall leaves or other plants in a basket on the altar to signify change.

2 Monday)) New moon in Virgo 9.55 pm EDT

Under this moon, cast for clarity and forgiveness of self. If you are too hard on yourself, set yourself a kinder new beginning.

3 Tuesday

Waxing

4 Wednesday

Waxing

5 Thursday

Waxing

6 Friday ◐

Waxing

7 Saturday ◐

Waxing

8 Sunday ◐

Waxing

Uphold the sacred boundary
of the self.

– THE GODDESS

M	T	W	T	F	S	S
						1
2	3	4	5	6	7	8
9	10	11	12	13	14	15
16	17	18	19	20	21	22
23	24	25	26	27	28	29
30						

SEPTEMBER

9 Monday

Waxing

10 Tuesday

Waxing

11 Wednesday

Waxing

12 Thursday

Waxing

13 Friday ◐

Waxing

14 Saturday ◐

Waxing

15 Sunday ◐

Waxing

SEPTEMBER						
M	T	W	T	F	S	S
						1
2	3	4	5	6	7	8
9	**10**	**11**	**12**	**13**	**14**	**15**
16	17	18	19	20	21	22
23	24	25	26	27	28	29
30						

16 Monday

Waxing

17 Tuesday Full moon in Pisces 10.34 pm EST

Super full moon and partial lunar eclipse visible in New York

Delight in a moon that brings harmony and understanding. This is a wonderful night for making aqua luna (moon water). Leave the purest water you can find in a white or silver bowl under the moon and retrieve and bottle prior to dawn. Use this in your potions, space clearing and even your bath!

18 Wednesday

Waning

Partial lunar eclipse visible in New York

19 Thursday

Waning

20 Friday ◑

Waning

21 Saturday ◑

Waning

22 Sunday ◑ Mabon, fall equinox, 8.43 am EDT

Waning

The hours of night and day are equal, then from tomorrow the days will grow shorter. The sunshine and warmth are receding day by day. Set intentions for health and life balance and to release what you don't need.

SEPTEMBER						
M	T	W	T	F	S	S
						1
2	3	4	5	6	7	8
9	10	11	12	13	14	15
16	**17**	**18**	**19**	**20**	**21**	**22**
23	24	25	26	27	28	29
30						

23 Monday ◑

Waning

24 Tuesday ◑

Waning

25 Wednesday ◑

Waning

26 Thursday ◑

Waning

27 Friday

Waning

28 Saturday

Waning

29 Sunday

Waning

Brightly you shine
When all that is not
needed is washed away.

- THE GODDESS

SEPTEMBER

M	T	W	T	F	S	S
						1
2	3	4	5	6	7	8
9	10	11	12	13	14	15
16	17	18	19	20	21	22
23	**24**	**25**	**26**	**27**	**28**	**29**
30						

OCTOBER

- What would I like to create, experience and manifest this month?

_____

_____

_____

_____

- What are the important dates for me this month?

_____

_____

- What would give me joy this month?

_____

_____

- What am I devoted to?

_____

_____

- Ideas, musings and actions:

_____

_____

_____

ANUBIS

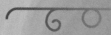

The majestic jackal-headed god Anubis stands next to an embalmer. He guides the embalmer's hands so they do the correct actions and listens in satisfaction as the correct incantations are made. Infinitely gentle, he takes great care of the tender new souls who have passed into the next world, the afterlife. He reassures them and makes them comfortable during their surprising journey to the goddess Maat, she who is law. It is Maat who will weigh their souls against the lightness of a feather and it is she who will determine whether these souls will live forever. Anubis will record this in the great Book of the Dead.

To our eyes Anubis perhaps looks fearsome, but this is not the truth. Although jackals did move among the graveyards and clear the dead, this jackal hopes that the person has lived a truthful and good life so they get to experience the afterlife. The alternative is that they get eaten by Ammut, the devourer of souls.

When the cult of the god Osiris grew stronger in the later Middle Kingdom of Egypt, Osiris took over many of Anubis's jobs as caretaker and protector of the dead. Thereafter, Anubis's myths became more focused on specific embalming methods and mummification processes. The care and effectiveness in which the mummification process was enacted is still a marvel today. The priests of the funerary rites would place a sacred mask of Anubis upon the deceaseds' faces when conducting the mummification so they thus became the god himself.

Prayer to Anubis for the Dead

This prayer to Anubis petitions him to take care of someone who has passed or is close to death. Should you have a fear of death you might also alter this for yourself.

Gather together: frankincense or myrrh resin ● a blue candle.

Burn the resin, light the candle and say:

'He who is on his mountain
He who is under his sand
He who is the place of embalming
He who is the steward of eternal life.
'Prepare [name of the person] for their journey
Watch over them
Teach them
Assuage their fear
Weigh their soul against Maat and may it be lighthearted
Show them mercy
And let them know your care and goodness.
'I ask that you watch over [name] and that their transition is easy and fearless.
I ask that you comfort the living who love them and
protect them while they are grieving.'
Let the candle safely burn down and thank Anubis.

THE WHEEL OF THE YEAR

Samhain

Happy witches' New Year! Yes, that is correct: Samhain (Hallowe'en) is in fact the beginning of our year. You might think it a strange phenomenon that this new beginning is linked with a creepy festival of death, but allow me to explain the reasoning.

Many pagans view this time as a void time, a time of pause that is full of possibility about the things to come rather than as a time for sadness or fear. If you imagine a fallow field, the land seemingly empty, resting, rejuvenating and waiting for and receptive to planting, this is how we see this time. We start with death and rest at the beginning of all things, and I personally believe this as a very rational, profound yet beautiful concept. Most folks do know that Samhain is a festival that celebrates death as a part of life, that it's not just about eating loads of pumpkin-spiced things. By doing this we smash a fair few taboos. We all will die, but until then we should celebrate the sweetness of life and not be unnecessarily afraid.

Samhain is an ancient Celtic festival that is linked to winter and reflects the seasonal harshness. In the traditional time it's held the season is moving towards winter and the dying back of earthly energy and the land is less productive. Our ancestors who lived in places where winter was extreme would have feared the season with its lack of food, less animals to hunt and more chance of disease.

HOW TO CELEBRATE SAMHAIN

I could write a book on the subject of how to celebrate Samhain, such is its rich traditions! As a witch I often get a lot of questions about trick or treating, such as why it is done. It was said that the spirits of the dead wandered the earth on Samhain night and trick or treating allowed people to explore death in a safe way. They could dress up as whatever they liked and wander undetected with the spirits, which couldn't tell they were alive and human. They could be as mischievous as they wanted to be if their candy wasn't forthcoming.

One of the traditions I always uphold is a meal with our benevolent ancestors wherein I invite them to enjoy the night with us. The table is always set beautifully, candles lit and music played. We feed our ancestors and give them good wine exactly as we are enjoying. We each tell stories of our ancestors and why they are special to us; in this way they are remembered and through this love death is transformed.

30 Monday ◗

Waning

1 Tuesday ●

Dark moon
Release and reflect

2 Wednesday ☽ New moon in Libra 2.49 pm EDT

Micro new moon
Delight in a new moon that is perfect for casting for happiness and beauty and the healing of old wounds.
Wednesday is named after the Norse god Wodin (Odin).

3 Thursday ◑

Waxing

4 Friday

Waxing

5 Saturday

Waxing

6 Sunday

Waxing

You carry the breath of your ancestors
Their blood, their determination
Yet there is only one you.

- THE GODDESS

SEPTEMBER						
M	T	W	T	F	S	S
						1
2	3	4	5	6	7	8
9	10	11	12	13	14	15
16	17	18	19	20	21	22
23	24	25	26	27	28	29
30						

OCTOBER

M	T	W	T	F	S	S
1	2	3	4	5	6	
7	8	9	10	11	12	13
14	15	16	17	18	19	20
21	22	23	24	25	26	27
28	29	30	31			

7 Monday ◐

Waxing

8 Tuesday ◐

Waxing

9 Wednesday ◐

Waxing

10 Thursday ◐

Waxing

11 Friday ◐

Waxing

12 Saturday ◐

Waxing

13 Sunday ◐

Waxing

OCTOBER
M T W T F S S

	1	2	3	4	5	6
7	**8**	**9**	**10**	**11**	**12**	**13**
14	15	16	17	18	19	20
21	22	23	24	25	26	27
28	29	30	31			

14 Monday

Waxing

15 Tuesday

Waxing

16 Wednesday

Waxing

17 Thursday ◯ Full moon in Aries 7.26 am EDT

Super full moon

This night is conducive to spells of protection and defence.

18 Friday 🌖

Waning

19 Saturday 🌖

Waning

20 Sunday 🌖

Waning

OCTOBER

M	T	W	T	F	S	S
		1	2	3	4	5	6
7	8	9	10	11	12	13
14	**15**	**16**	**17**	**18**	**19**	**20**
21	22	23	24	25	26	27
28	29	30	31			

21 Monday ☽

Waning

22 Tuesday ☽

Waning

23 Wednesday ☽

Waning

24 Thursday ☽

Waning

25 Friday ☽

Waning

26 Saturday ☽

Waning

27 Sunday ☽

Waning

OCTOBER

M	T	W	T	F	S	S
		1	2	3	4	5	6
7	8	9	10	11	12	13
14	15	16	17	18	19	20
21	**22**	**23**	**24**	**25**	**26**	**27**
28	29	30	31			

28 Monday

Waning

29 Tuesday

Waning

30 Wednesday

Waning

31 Thursday

Dark moon

It's Samhain: happy witches' New Year and an extra-special dark moon Hallowe'en! This is the celebration of seeing death as being just another part of life. This is one of the two nights of the year where the veil between the worlds is at its thinnest, so it's a great night for divination of all kinds. Feast with your friends and don't forget those who have passed: set a place for them, pour them wine, leave them delicious food and speak about them!

1 Friday 🌙 New moon in Scorpio 8.47 am EST

Get in touch with pleasure again: set intentions for more joy and fun.

2 Saturday

Waxing

3 Sunday

Waxing

The spiral turns
Sometimes inwards
Sometimes outwards
Changing always.

– THE GODDESS

OCTOBER							NOVEMBER						
M	**T**	**W**	**T**	**F**	**S**	**S**	**M**	**T**	**W**	**T**	**F**	**S**	**S**
	1	2	3	4	5	6					1	2	3
7	8	9	10	11	12	13	4	5	6	7	8	9	10
14	15	16	17	18	19	20	11	12	13	14	15	16	17
21	22	23	24	25	26	27	18	19	20	21	22	23	24
28	**29**	**30**	**31**				25	26	27	28	29	30	

NOVEMBER

- ◆ What would I like to create, experience and manifest this month?

_____

_____

_____

_____

- ◆ What are the important dates for me this month?

_____

_____

- ◆ What would give me joy this month?

_____

_____

- ◆ What am I devoted to?

_____

_____

- ◆ Ideas, musings and actions:

_____

_____

_____

HYPNOS

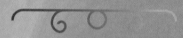

If there is an ancient god who many people need the help of right now it's Hypnos, the Greek god of sound sleep. Hypnos was born from the dark mother Nyx (night). A twin, he was often pictured hand in hand with his brother Thanatos (death) and the brothers shadowed each other in their work.

While featuring in a number of myths, Hypnos was generally seen as a benevolent and relief-inducing deity and was honored for his place in well-being and health. One story in which Hera bribed Hypnos to practice his arts on Zeus so that her favored Heracles got to make yet another outrageous escape in return for a beautiful bride is about as rebellious as Hypnos got.

Our world is busier than ever and sometimes finding a decent night's sleep can be difficult. Hypnos can always be called upon to assist in times when stress, travel, work or insomnia has robbed you of your sleep. In our modern lives there is another time that Hypnos's favor should be courted, and that is in anesthesia. If you are undergoing an operation why not give a little libation to Hypnos prior to the procedure, as it is Hypnos who will be guiding the hand of your anesthetic doctor as he artfully sends you into painless sleep.

Ritual for peaceful sleep

This is a lovely ritual to do when you are feeling a little hyper too close to bedtime or cannot sleep.

Gather together: 1 teaspoonful of chamomile tea • some lemon balm or rose geranium leaves • a candle of any color • a pen and some paper • a basket with a lid.

Steep together the chamomile tea and lemon balm in a pot of hot water.

Light the candle and place it
beside a bath or shower and say:

*'Great god Hypnos, king of sleep, god of the peaceful
dreams, ensure my sleep is deep tonight!'*

Run a warm bath or shower and relax in this for a while. Do not read in the bath or be stimulated by any media in any way. Get out of the bath and drink the tea; these herbs are very calming for the body and mind.

Write down anything that is making you anxious or worried or that represents pressure for you. No essays; just short point form, please. Put the list in the basket and place it along with the candle somewhere in your bedroom but not on the bedside table or too close to the bed.

Just before getting into bed, say:

*'I place these here, they will not interfere
With my sleep tonight, I will wake up bright!'*

Blow out the candle and go to bed, knowing that you are looked after and that peaceful sleep awaits. Happy dreams!

4 Monday ☽

Waxing

5 Tuesday ☽

Waxing

6 Wednesday ☽

Waxing

7 Thursday ☽

Waxing

8 Friday 🌓

Waxing

9 Saturday 🌓

Waxing

10 Sunday 🌓

Waxing

NOVEMBER

M	T	W	T	F	S	S
				1	2	3
4	**5**	**6**	**7**	**8**	**9**	**10**
11	12	13	14	15	16	17
18	19	20	21	22	23	24
25	26	27	28	29	30	

11 Monday ◗

Waxing

Harvest above-ground fruits and vegetables now.

12 Tuesday ◗

Waxing

13 Wednesday ◗

Waxing

14 Thursday ◗

Waxing

15 Friday ○ Full moon in Taurus 4.28 pm EST

Cast for a new home or better living situation. Set intentions for your own strength and growth.

16 Saturday ◐

Waning

17 Sunday ◐

Waning

NOVEMBER

M	T	W	T	F	S	S
				1	2	3
4	5	6	7	8	9	10
11	**12**	**13**	**14**	**15**	**16**	**17**
18	19	20	21	22	23	24
25	26	27	28	29	30	

18 Monday ◑

Waning

19 Tuesday ◑

Waning

20 Wednesday ◑

Waning

21 Thursday ◑

Waning

22 Friday ◑

Waning

23 Saturday ◑

Waning

24 Sunday ◑

Waning

NOVEMBER

M	T	W	T	F	S	S
				1	2	3
4	5	6	7	8	9	10
11	12	13	14	15	16	17
18	**19**	**20**	**21**	**22**	**23**	**24**
25	26	27	28	29	30	

25 Monday ◐

Waning

Trim your hair now if you wish to encourage growth.

26 Tuesday ◐

Waning

27 Wednesday ◐

Waning

28 Thursday ◐

Waning

29 Friday

Waning

30 Saturday

Dark moon

Rest and restore and allow grudges to be lifted.

1 Sunday ☽ New moon in Sagittarius 1.21 am EST

Perhaps cast with some friends for goals and wishes. This is a moon to set intentions for personal freedom and happiness.

NOVEMBER							DECEMBER						
M	**T**	**W**	**T**	**F**	**S**	**S**	M	T	W	T	F	S	S
				1	2	3							1
4	5	6	7	8	9	10	2	3	4	5	6	7	8
11	12	13	14	15	16	17	9	10	11	12	13	14	15
18	19	20	21	22	23	24	16	17	18	19	20	21	22
25	**26**	**27**	**28**	**29**	**30**		23	24	25	26	27	28	29
							30	31					

DECEMBER

- ◆ What would I like to create, experience and manifest this month?

_____

_____

_____

_____

- ◆ What are the important dates for me this month?

_____

_____

- ◆ What would give me joy this month?

_____

_____

- ◆ What am I devoted to?

_____

_____

- ◆ Ideas, musings and actions:

_____

_____

_____

WINTER

The magic of slowing down

In winter all the growth processes of the earth slow down. The shorter days and lower temperatures are a kind of pause, and everything becomes much more introverted and contracted. Energy reduces, the withdrawal being part of the natural cycle. If it's not resisted this withdrawal can be ultimately pleasant and health giving. We can take this time to slow down, dream, restore ourselves and even catch up on our sleep. We might spend more time indoors, a kind of cocooning that again is absolutely part of a natural seasonal cycle.

As humans we are part of the great circle of seasons, animals, biomes and elements. If we align ourselves with the cycles we will be healthier in body, mind and spirit, which means we should eat differently, act differently, expend energy differently and even cast differently. In the extreme seasons, this is even more important.

For me winter doesn't mean I do nothing, but it does mean I plan. I habitually plan for my business during this time and I take time out to dream of what could be. I exercise differently and try to find the snow to play in. I cook more and am more mindful of taking care of my body. I don't let it become so still that it becomes stagnant, but I ensure I get plenty of rest on the long dark nights.

Working with the dark gods and goddesses is ideal during the long nights of winter. Everyone needs to do work on their shadow self, and winter is a great time for this.

Embracing the Dark Ritual

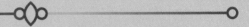

AHEAD OF TIME, THINK ABOUT YOUR SHADOW SELF, THE PART OF
YOU THAT YOU MIGHT WISH TO ACCEPT MORE OR, ALTERNATIVELY,
IMPROVE. THINK ABOUT THIS BEFORE YOU DO THE RITUAL. IT IS ALSO
VITAL THAT YOU DO THIS RITUAL IN THE DARK, WHICH MAY MEAN
SOMEWHERE IN YOUR HOME OR OUTSIDE UNDER THE NIGHT SKY.

Gather together: a torch • a small, dark-colored crystal such as jet or obsidian or even a dark river stone • a dark-colored candle • a pen and some paper.

Sit down in the dark with the torch turned off. Keeping your eyes open, breathe deeply and center yourself.

SAY:

'I welcome in the friendly darkness. I welcome in my shadow self.'

Feel the darkness: does it have a smell, feeling or sound? Does it have a temperature? Feel with *all* of your senses. Think about your personal shadow self: what is it that you wish to change or cannot accept? Think about what specifically your shadow self may have cost you; for example, peace of mind, that you don't do certain things that you might like to and so on. These feelings may not be pleasant, which is fine as you'll be releasing them.

Hold the crystal in your hand and allow your feelings to fuse into the stone. State out aloud what it is you might wish to accept or release or improve about your shadow self; for example, *'I do not have strong self-esteem'*, *'I don't trust myself'*, *'It has cost me peace of mind/opportunities/happiness!'*

SAY:

'I release these to the stone and to the darkness to be recycled into what now serves me!'

LIGHT THE CANDLE AND SAY:

'I accept change and accept myself yet allow what needs to die to die.'

Ask the universe if there is anything it wishes to tell you that will enable you to take action and allow any messages to come to mind. Write them down; you can action them later.

Blow out the candle and give thanks. So it will be as you have asked!

HATHOR

In December most people try to see the light at the end of the tunnel of the year and begin to consider that we have a month to go before hopefully getting a breather. We might see family during that holiday time or we might get together with friends and party. We might even decide to take a solo break and simply relax a little.

Whatever you decide to do it's worth making sure you find some pleasure in it, and Hathor is just the goddess to help you with this. She was one of the most-loved deities in Ancient Egypt, and if you venture into modern Egypt and visit well-known temples and tombs of this ancient race you'll find the cow-horned, crowned Hathor featuring widely in sculptures and paintings.

Hathor is quite an easy deity to identify among the many that are presented as she is often pictured as a beautiful woman with the ears of a cow or wearing cow horns with the sun balanced between them. In later depictions she is seen with the entire head of a cow. The cow symbology is a hint at her area of influence. Think of the animal: its soft eyes, its contented demeanor and its role in fertility and maternal nourishment. Hathor's contented and happy influence extended to all things that give joy, such as music, dancing, sex and even drunkenness!

The temples of Hathor were joyful places full of songs, dance and beauty. There were even small temples in her honor situated outside those of major deities so that people could be in a happy and contented mental mood before entering to worship. The Egyptians clearly believed that having a positive or relaxed state of mind assisted in having a positive spiritual connection.

Call upon Hathor when you most need to find joyful peace in your life. When you are feeling chaotic, ungrounded or unhappy, her steadying influence of contentment is energy that is always welcome. Hathor's energy is loving yet strong and celebrates the fullness and nourishing power that comes with being fulfilled and satisfied. If you feel very driven all the time you may find sanctuary within her influence.

INVOCATION FOR JOY AND CONTENTMENT

IF YOU WOULD LIKE TO BRING MORE PEACEFUL
CONTENTMENT INTO YOUR LIFE AND A BIT MORE PLEASURE
YOU MIGHT LIKE TO TRY THIS INVOCATION.

Gather together: a white candle • 4 small pieces of
turquoise or lapis lazuli • some small bells.

Light the candle and hold the stones in your hand.
Breathe in and think about a time in your life
when you felt peaceful and contented.

BREATHE IN AGAIN AND PUMP UP THIS FEELING,
THEN WHEN IT IS VERY STRONG WITHIN YOU SAY:

'Hathor, lady of amenity, the dweller in the great land, give me joy!

'Hathor, cow-eyed mother of the pharaoh, give me happiness!

'Hathor, the lady of Ta-tchesert, the eye of Ra, grant me contentment!

*'Bless these stones I have in my hand, bring your blessing of joy, love, nourishment
and satisfaction to them and allowing them to be a talisman of good fortune.'*

Place one stone in each corner of your home, thanking Hathor as you leave
each one and jingling the bells. This will grid your home in her energy.

Blow out the candle and give thanks.

THE WHEEL OF THE YEAR

Yule: winter solstice

21 December 4.20 am EST

Yule (Yul) is what Christmas is called in many places in Scandinavia and Europe. If you have ever spent any time around Christmas in those places you'll appreciate that it is a living, breathing tradition.

Why is Yule associated with Christmas? Yul was originally a Norse solstice festival celebrating the return of the light after the longest night of the year that overlapped the Christian tradition of Christmas. The festival at its heart engages with the idea of the birth of light and hope over darkness from this night onwards, the daylight hours growing incrementally each day and warmth returning to the earth. For our ancient ancestors this returning of the light after the depth and death of winter was a wonderful thing!

The symbology of Yule is something everyone knows: the tree, gifts, feasting and the Yule log. The tree symbolises the returning of fertility to nature and bringing the outside in again, while gifts were talismans for prosperity, fecundity and luck: something everyone needed! Feasting was undertaken because with the light returning there was cause for celebration and stores of food could be used. The famous Yule log was used to convey hopes for the future and ritually burned to release those wishes.

In ancient times communal fires were lit that could be seen right across the landscape for all to be cheered by. The ashes of the fires were used in other workings later in the year.

HOW TO CELEBRATE YULE

The first thing to source is the Yule log. I go out to my garden or friends' gardens to seek out a branch or section of a tree that has already been discarded. If at all possible you shouldn't cut anything off a living tree.

Prepare some small slips of paper for you and your guests to write their hopeful wishes on. Really consider these carefully, as this is a powerfully magical night for wish manifestation so don't waste it! Pin the wishes on the log or make slits in it to hold the paper. Your log should be covered in amazing wishes and look quite pretty. Start a fire in a hearth or open fire pit and stoke it so it is hot and roaring. Gather everyone around with their mulled wine and together throw the log in the fire. Everyone can sing or tell each other of their wish and be encouraged, but whatever you do make sure you cheer the burning!

2 Monday ◑

Waxing

3 Tuesday ◑

Waxing

4 Wednesday ◑

Waxing

5 Thursday ◑

Waxing

6 Friday

Waxing

7 Saturday

Waxing

8 Sunday

Waxing

Look at the slim crescent in the sky
Don't we always get a fresh start?

- THE GODDESS

DECEMBER

M	T	W	T	F	S	S
						1
2	3	4	5	6	7	8
9	10	11	12	13	14	15
16	17	18	19	20	21	22
23	24	25	26	27	28	29
30	31					

9 Monday

Waxing

10 Tuesday

Waxing

11 Wednesday

Waxing

12 Thursday

Waxing

13 Friday

Waxing

14 Saturday

Waxing

15 Sunday ○ Full moon in Gemini 4.01 am EST

This is a night to cast for big things, although a little structure is not a bad thing. We are almost at the end of 2024, so you might like to use this lunar event to lightly plan your next moves.

The first organising principal in the
universe is love.

– THE GODDESS

DECEMBER

M	T	W	T	F	S	S
						1
2	3	4	5	6	7	8
9	**10**	**11**	**12**	**13**	**14**	**15**
16	17	18	19	20	21	22
23	24	25	26	27	28	29
30	31					

16 Monday

Waning

17 Tuesday

Waning

18 Wednesday

Waning

19 Thursday

Waning

20 Friday

Waning

21 Saturday Yule, winter solstice, 4.20 am EST

Waning

This is a beautiful festival of hope and light. Prepare a yule log and pin your wishes upon it, make mulled wine and feast with friends. Prepare talismans as gifts to attract prosperity and joy.

22 Sunday

Waning

It's heavy
This burden
Set it down my child
And we will see if it's worth picking back up.

– THE GODDESS

DECEMBER

M	T	W	T	F	S	S
						1
2	3	4	5	6	7	8
9	10	11	12	13	14	15
16	**17**	**18**	**19**	**20**	**21**	**22**
23	24	25	26	27	28	29
30	31					

23 Monday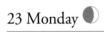

Waning

24 Tuesday

Waning

Christmas Eve

25 Wednesday

Waning

Christmas Day

26 Thursday

Waning

27 Friday ◑

Waning

28 Saturday ◑

Waning

29 Sunday ●

Dark moon

This is the last dark moon for the year and is also a black moon (the second new moon in one calendar month). Cut cords with events, people or relationships that no longer serve you or support your future.

Authentic and whole:
I made you wildly, purposefully
That way.

- THE GODDESS

DECEMBER						
M	**T**	**W**	**T**	**F**	**S**	**S**
						1
2	3	4	5	6	7	8
9	10	11	12	13	14	15
16	17	18	19	20	21	22
23	**24**	**25**	**26**	**27**	**28**	**29**
30	31					

30 Monday New moon in Capricorn 5.26 pm EST

Here is your chance to cast for all you want in 2025, especially what needs to begin anew or start. Cast for the success of fresh projects and endeavors.

31 Tuesday

Waxing

Say goodbye to 2024! It's the final night of this year, so ride the positive wave of wishes for the new year. Take big breaths in and out and mark the moment with a kiss, dance or sip of champagne. Spill a little on the ground for the goddess of the new near, Jana, as the clock moves towards midnight.

Check Stacey Demarco on Facebook for the free annual Ride the Wave Ritual Event. Let go of what was and ready yourself for new momentum, ensure you have your intentions set for 2025! Mark the end of this year with a ritual of gratitude before you head out to celebrate.

1 Wednesday

Waxing

Welcome to 2025!

2 Thursday

Waxing

3 Friday ◗

Waxing

4 Saturday ◑

Waxing

5 Sunday ◑

Waxing

DECEMBER							JANUARY			2025			
M	**T**	**W**	**T**	**F**	**S**	**S**	M	T	W	T	F	S	S
						1		**1**	**2**	**3**	**4**	**5**	
2	3	4	5	6	7	8	6	7	8	9	10	11	12
9	10	11	12	13	14	15	13	14	15	16	17	18	19
16	17	18	19	20	21	22	20	21	22	23	24	25	26
23	24	25	26	27	28	29	27	28	29	30	31		
30	**31**												

MY ACHIEVEMENTS AND HIGHLIGHTS FOR 2024

NOTES AND MUSINGS

2024 MOON PHASES

UNIVERSAL TIME CHART

This handy chart gives moon phases in universal time (UT). It is the mean solar time for the meridian at Greenwich, England, and is used as a basis for calculating time throughout most of the world.

DARK MOON	NEW MOON	FULL MOON
10 January	11 January, 11.57 am	25 January, 5.54 pm
8 February	9 February, 10.59 pm	24 February, 12.30 pm
9 March	10 March, 9.00 am	25 March, 7.00 am
7 April	8 April, 7.20 pm	24 April, 12.48 am
7 May	8 May, 4.21 am	23 May, 2.53 pm
5 June	6 June, 1.37 pm	22 June, 2.07 am
4 July	5 July, 11.57 pm	21 July, 11.17 am
3 August	4 August, 12.13 pm	19 August, 7.25 pm
2 September	3 September, 2.55 am	18 September, 3.34 am
1 October	2 October, 7.49 pm	17 October, 12.26 pm
31 October	1 November, 12.47 pm	15 November, 9.28 pm
30 November	1 December, 6.21 am	15 December, 9.01 am
29 December	30 December, 10.26 pm	—

RESOURCES

Here is a list of handy moon, earth and pagan-related resources that I particularly like.

The Pagan Awareness Network

www.paganawareness.net.au: if you want more information on paganism or witchcraft this is a great place to start. The Pagan Awareness Network Incorporated (PAN Inc) is a not-for-profit educational association with members Australia-wide. It is directed by a management committee whose members are drawn from a broad cross-section of the pagan community. It has no formal ties with any religious body but works proactively both within the pagan community and as a point of contact for the public, including government and media organisations. PAN Inc aims to continue as the Australian pagan community's most effective networking and educational body.

www.themodernwitch.com: my website contains loads of free resources, witches' tools, free downloads and a store from which you can obtain books, downloads, blessed talismans and temple beads including lunar beads. Register for the free newsletter.

www.natureluster.com: this is my site about the benefits and wonders of an earth-centered life. Try the Natureluster Programme; search for Natureluster on Instagram.

LUNAR WEBSITES

- *http://eclipse.gsfc.nasa.gov/phase/phasecat.html:* is a NASA site that provides a great history and current info about moon phases. It is wonderful for researching your lunar return.
- *www.timeanddate.com:* this website is great for lunar timing and equinox information.

TIDAL INFORMATION

Strangely enough, some of the best tidal information comes from your popular newspapers; for example, in Australia *The Sydney Morning Herald* and *The Age*.

Try *www.smh.com.au* OR *www.theage.com.au.*

For moon gardening: *www.green-change.com* OR *www.moongardeningcalendar.com.*

CONNECT WITH ME

Connect with Stacey Demarco: *www.facebook.com/staceydemarco*

The 5000: *www.facebook.com/The5000*

Instagram: *The Modern Witch* AND *Natureluster*

ABOUT THE AUTHOR

Stacey Demarco is The Modern Witch. Passionate about bringing practical magic to everyone and inspiring people to have a deeper connection with nature, she has been teaching witchcraft and mythos for many decades. This diary is now in its 14th edition and is published in both the southern and northern hemispheres.

Stacey is the author of the bestsellers *Witch in the Boardroom*, *Witch in the Bedroom*, *The Enchanted Moon* and *The Priestess Path*, all of which have been translated into other languages. She is the co-writer of *The No Excuses Guide to Soulmates*, *The No Excuses Guide to Purpose* and *Plants of Power*. Her oracle card decks include the bestselling *Queen of the Moon*, *Divine Animals*, *Moon Magick*, *Elemental Oracle* and *Deep, Dark and Dangerous*, all illustrated by Kinga Britschgi.

Stacey is the founder of Natureluster, which educates and works to reconnect people to the health-giving power of nature.

An animal activist, ethical beekeeper and dedicated adventure traveler, she lives in Sydney, Australia on a cliff by the beach with her husband and furry companions. Stacey provides private consults as well as teaching workshops, and leads the popular Wild Souls Retreats nationally and internationally.

Learn more at *www.themodernwitch.com* or join her on Facebook.